A Few Things Before I Go

Patrick McKenna

Library of Congress Control Number: 2020915865

ISBN 9780578779713

For

Anne Elizabeth McKenna
&
John Harlan McKenna

It could not be otherwise.

➤ CONTENTS

➢ EDITOR'S NOTE

It's rare for an editor to take on a project from a stranger and wind up with a new friend. It is rarer still to have this friend become a source of hope and light during the dark months of the Covid-19 pandemic. But that's what happened when I was introduced to Patrick McKenna via email in December of 2019 and agreed to take on this project. And I believe any reader of *A Few Things Before I Go* will walk away with those benefits as well.

Patrick wrote this book in the final, grueling stages of ALS, a pitiless disease that, by the time we met, had robbed him of his ability to speak, to write and to type, but had clearly not diminished his wry sense of humor, sharp intelligence, warmth and opinionated world-view. Patrick is a man who knows what he wants, and right off the bat, he told me he aimed to create a "small, pamphlet-sized" book of business and life advice for his two almost-grown children, Anne and Jack. He would do this, he informed me, using the power of eye gaze technology, without touching a single key or lifting a pencil. I was intrigued, and a tad skeptical: *Should a book from a dying man to his kids really be about business?* I wondered. *Shouldn't it be more emotional?* I was also a bit worried that the project would be depressing because, well, ALS.

Instead, I began to look forward to Patrick's pages and his snappy emails with eager anticipation—his anecdotes about being a sometimes overconfident law student and young lawyer; the reflections on fatherhood and where he succeeded and fell short; the unabashed spirituality that ended up shaping his outlook (including an adolescent religious awakening of sorts that took place in a headshop in Schenectady, New York). With my urging, he also agreed to tap into some unexpected emotions, and talk about what it took to cope with, survive and even thrive after his life-changing diagnosis. And so, while Patrick does indeed dole out smart advice on everything from closing a deal to acing a presentation, this book is so much more than a business book. To my mind, *A Few Things Before I Go* is the ultimate lesson on how to live well and how to die well, with gratitude, honesty, and a clear-eyed perspective on what it means to be a good person. These pages are brimming with hope, humor and wise advice that will stay with his two children, his loved ones, and anyone else lucky enough to hold this slim volume in their hands.

Whenever I felt trapped and despairing during the spring and summer of 2020, unable to travel or see friends or hug or share a meal with those I love best because of the pandemic, I'd find myself thinking of Patrick, a man who was truly "locked down" yet who managed to lift me up. I know this book will lift readers, too, and give them a guide for living and loving and seizing the moment, whatever their situation or the state of their health. Because as Patrick demonstrates in every single line, the moment is truly all we have.

—Paula Derrow July 13, 2020

➤ PREFACE

This book is based on 58 years of living, working, and learning. Some of what's in here may seem basic, but as I look back, I'm amazed at how many times I've had to relearn the same lessons. My hope is that by sharing this, I might save you from making my missteps and help your lives be a little easier.

I originally envisioned this as a memo filled with professional advice for an audience of two, but I discovered that it was impossible to avoid veering into very personal territory. See, with my days numbered, my mind plays this trick where an idea, or a poem, or a favorite quip pops up and I think, "Ooh! I'd better include that, too! Wouldn't it be a shame if that gem was lost?" Hubris? Yeah.

And then Covid-19 happened. Suddenly, the world was in lockdown with me, but like everyone else, I found it difficult to concentrate, to focus. I felt I could offer nothing you'd find useful in any of the dystopian versions of the future my mind conjured. And so, I took a two-week break in the middle of this project. I imagined my eyes would benefit from taking a hiatus from eye-gaze typing for 10 hours at a stretch. But two weeks passed, and my eyes got wonky and even harder to focus. Lou Gehrig's disease isn't just progressive, it's relentless. I so wanted ALS to give me a little break, to level off for a week while I got caught up. But no.

Funnily enough, that taught me something that (not surprisingly) I'm going to pass on to you, along with the other advice in this book. Sometimes, survival, much less living the life we expected to live, simply isn't possible. Failing to acknowledge that is itself a failure to face the brutal truth of one's situation. How, then, is one able to not lose hope when death is the inevitable outcome? In this case, I've discovered that it's about learning to define success as something other than living and about having objectives that are both positive and attainable.

My hope is that this book gets you closer to being able to accomplish that. And lest you think I've changed too much, I've still got my perhaps inflated sense of pride, as evidenced by the ISBN bar code I'm including on the back of this volume, along with the Library of Congress registration number near the copyright. Who adds those to a memo to their kids? Let's just be kind and say that I am someone with great self-confidence. I'm going to print about 100 of these as I've had several requests for copies, and I want you to have extras to give away.

The ISBN number is needed if you decide you want to market this to a wider audience. (There may very well be one, since top companies and captains of industry paid me a lot of money for my advice and coaching.) Plus, some people ascribe an extra wisdom dividend to the words of a dying person. I don't know about that, but what I do know is that nothing focuses the mind like the ultimate deadline.

P.S. I think the Library of Congress number is optional. Put it in the same vanity bucket as my admission to the Supreme Court, the judge's badge, and the Actor's Equity membership. This used to be known as a humblebrag, but I am reliably informed by Ashley Engelman, and this was confirmed by you, Jack, that it's now called a flex (!). I'm flexing.

➤ M-E-M-O-R-A-N-D-U-M[1]

TO: Anne and Jack
FROM: Dad
SUBJ: A few things before I go
DATE: March 15, 2020

After my diagnosis with Lou Gehrig's disease, I spent a long time waffling between wet and dry eyes while deciding what to write to you.

When I tried writing about big truths, such as *You are enough just as you are,* or focused on my feelings, like how proud I am of you, or how I hope you'll forgive me for pain I've caused, I discovered that my efforts simply made my eyes wet. And when using eye-gaze technology, typing a cogent sentence through tears takes pretty much forever.

I don't have forever. So, I made a few adjustments. I decided that a drier-eyed solution would be to tell you about the insights that have accounted for much of my happiness and success, personal and professional. In the first part of the book, I offer mostly straight business advice with personal asides and lessons flowing from that advice. About two-thirds of the way through, after Covid-19 hit, I

---

[1] This memorandum was the original preface before the "end" was clear in my mind.

decided I would tell the stories first and let any learnings flow from them, which I realized would improve my chances of finishing this damn thing before the deadline.

My reason for writing this book, however, remains the same: I'm writing this because I love you and want to make something useful that you can look back on years from now in case you ever find yourself saying, "I wonder what Dad would have said?" My hope is that at those times, you'll dust off the book, crack it open, and feel like I am sitting next to you, offering too many ideas (and too much nagging!) to help. In other words, you'll feel that nothing has changed!

This book contains my best advice, as well as tips from others I respect, on how I believe relationships should be built, along with some ideas about how to build an authentic foundation for your adult lives. You'll also find a bunch of specific advice on communicating, suitable for many situations, that I picked up over my career. If you use these tools, they will yield big dividends, especially early on. They have been field-tested and will get your careers—and your relationships—off on the right foot.

But first, I just want to say this. For posterity:

Anne, Jack, I love you, and each one of you is enough just as you are;

I am over-the-moon proud of you both;

Forgiveness is, indeed, a powerful and beautiful thing. Thank you.

What I wanted most in life was to be your dad, and you guys brought me the greatest joy I've known. I'm "well pleased" that so much of what I hold to be right and good manifests in both of you—your commitment to fighting climate change and to justice, race and gender issues, as well as sticking up for the disadvantaged. I couldn't ask for a better legacy than both of you, but even more important, you will doubtless enjoy fulfilling lives, and there is no more peaceful thought for me than that.

CHAPTER 1

The Art of Balance

S hortly after my dad passed away, I was cleaning out his office at Siena College when I came across a collection of the poetry of Robert Frost, where I found these words:

> *My object in living is to unite*
> *My avocation and my vocation*
> *As my two eyes make one in sight.*
> *Only where love and need are one,*
> *And the work is play for mortal stakes,*
> *Is the deed ever really done*
> *For Heaven and the future's sakes.*
> *—Robert Frost, "Two Tramps in Mud Time"*

At the time, I was working at the American Cancer Society, and my vocation did indeed feel like a favorite hobby. I was fortunate that my work held such meaning—we were literally curing cancer.

I know that you two will come to your own unique ways of finding meaning in your work. It's a pretty natural process if you can answer four questions: *What do you love? What are you good at? What does the world need?* And, a more prosaic question, but to my mind, equally necessary: *What can you get paid for?*

Both of you are young and smart and have strong beliefs. All good. Just know that people who feel super passionate or "called" to their careers also tend to have high rates of burnout.

If you find yourself with a passion for your work, or even a sense of obligation or moral duty to do something, that's wonderful—few people in life can say that. But you must also be vigilant about not letting your job knock you off the work/life balance beam. Do as I say, not as I did, ok?

There is a lot more to life than work, including tending to your families and keeping engaged with your friends and the activities that fulfill you. If fitting all of that in seems difficult, ask for help when you need it, and give help as generously when asked.

To me, balance is crucial. And I believe that balance begins with authenticity. By the time I started law school, my goal going forward was simply to become more authentic, meaning that I wanted to be me—to believe that I was good enough, and to stop trying to please everyone. That wasn't an easy task. The day I received my law school acceptance letter, I went to the gym and had a full-on panic attack—I was convinced I would fail out and be buried in debt. I exhausted myself and ended up panic napping on a yoga mat for about an hour. It took a long time for me to overcome imposter syndrome, but eventually I did. I learned that whether I was at home or at work, I didn't need to change my persona.

> CHAPTER 2

Acknowledge a Power Greater Than Yourself

One thing that helped me get to authenticity, ironically, was putting aside my pride and realizing that the world didn't begin and end with me. In other words, it's important to acknowledge a power greater than yourself. You can have as heavy or light a schedule of spirit-enriching practices as you want, but even if you consider yourself an atheist, I think this is crucial. For one thing, believing in a higher power helps to keep the ego in check. It also ensures that you don't take yourself too seriously.

By the time I limped through the 1980s, having exhausted all the vices for which that decade was known, I realized, quite by surprise, that my life lacked any spiritual dimension. I also seemed to have missed developing the habit of self-reflection, let alone doing it with a clear head.

Then something happened that made it plain to me that I needed a spiritual component in my life if I wanted to create and sustain meaningful relationships. I had recently changed jobs to a position where I was doing fundraising with a large United Cerebral Palsy chapter. There, I was asked to adopt the Franklin time-management system, which involved watching a four-hour video of Stephen Covey explaining how the process would benefit all of life's dimensions. The chart below sums it up quite well:

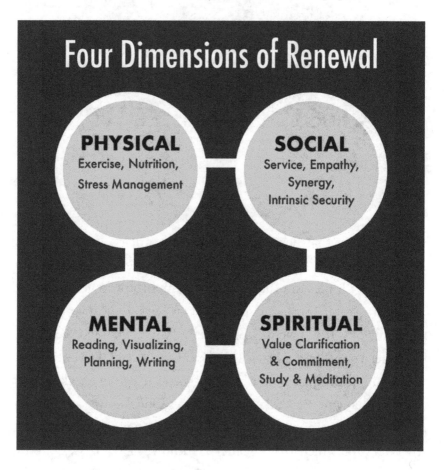

At first, I was delighted. I knew intuitively that this system would benefit me. I had great ideas about how I would revitalize the physical, social, and mental areas of my life.

But when asked to consider my own spiritual dimension, I had an "oh, shit!" moment. This Covey guy wasn't recruiting for the Mormons. He wasn't even pushing organized religion. He was happy if people considered contemplating trees as the entirety of their spiritual life. The bar could not have been any lower. And still, I sat on the couch, dumbstruck, realizing I had no spiritual life whatsoever.

At that moment, I vowed to change all that. I found this method of getting control of one's life so compelling, and I was so sick and tired of this unshakable sense I had that my life was in a downward spiral, that I decided to get myself a spiritual life. That evening, I enthusiastically explained all this to my fiancée, and she responded with a blank stare, then lit a joint.

We never did get married.

Instead, in my late 20s, I began my search for spirituality by returning to my spiritual roots. I was raised Catholic, so I started there, then made the rounds with other denominations.[2]

---

[2] I was born Roman Catholic. My dad's sister, Mary, was a nun, and I found that I liked the majesty of cathedrals, the sound of the organ, the smell of incense. And, goodness, there is no better way to be ushered out of this world and into the next than with a majestic Catholic funeral. And while I doubt that I'll have a funeral mass, I'm leaning toward taking the sacrament of *extreme unction*. As far as the Catholics are concerned, once baptized, you never really leave home.

Ultimately, however, the problems of the Roman Catholic church—among them the exclusion of women clergy and the criminal cover-up of child sex abuse, not to mention the ubiquity of folk guitars—made staying untenable for me.

That's when I became a Presbyterian. For me, it was a better fit and I liked the people. I also liked what I saw as a pronounced preference for wrestling with text and teachings rather than looking to the Bible for black-and-white answers. But my primary focus during those years was to exercise the leadership skills that had remained dormant as I toiled away as an associate at a law firm. I became an elder and, upon completing a two-year-long training, a Lay Pastor, filling in as preacher for churches between full-time pastors. I was broadly fulfilled by being able to apply my newly-developed leadership skills to support my liberal congregation in battling (a nice Christian verb!) the conservative/evangelical side over the ordination of gay men and lesbians.

Yet inside, I still felt a sense of unease…or inauthenticity. When you two were baptized, I remember the pastor asking me if I renounced Satan. I knew I was

Ultimately, I found my conception of God not in a church, exactly, but in a church basement, where many 12-step groups meet. Since their inception in the 1930s, the 12-step movement has directed its members to surrender to God. Of course, that left out atheists and agnostics who might object to the explicit God reference, and so someone humbly suggested that God be defined simply as a power greater than ourselves.

I recognized this sense of a higher power immediately. Basically, the message was: None of us is God. It was like running into an old friend—in this case, a friend I first met when I was about 12 years old, in a head shop in Schenectady, New York, of all places.

➤ The Desiderata

It was with studied nonchalance that I entered that head shop, with the same objective as always: to see if there were any new posters of scantily clad women. I sidled to the back where the posters were located, flanked on either side by a wall display of sex toys (which I was too embarrassed to look at) and a showcase of "smoking accessories" (which I was too scared to be seen looking at).

In my 12-year-old mind, perusing posters was a justifiable activity because the subjects extended to such things as race cars

---

supposed to say yes, and I did. But if I'm honest, I was thinking, "Satan? Really? Well, sure. Why not?" Not much authenticity there! So, ultimately, organized religion didn't provide a foundation for the authentic life I was seeking.

I also studied Eastern philosophy; did some deep reading on metaphysical Christianity; attended a Methodist church; and dabbled in some New Age spirituality, including A Course in Miracles as well as Eckhart Tolle. Nothing stuck. Despite my efforts, I couldn't find a religion that suited me. Yet despite the influence of my Vermont Yankee mother, I didn't believe in complete self-reliance, though I found a lot to recommend in the Stoic philosophy. What I did know is that I was a spiritual being on a human journey.

and kittens holding on to the end of ropes, which acted as a kind of camouflage for my real goal: flipping through images of half-naked movie stars. And so I was obliged to assume the demeanor of an art gallery patron and take my time examining each poster, rather than flipping straight to the women.

Which is how I discovered the Desiderata, a prose poem written in 1927 by Max Ehrmann, a poet and lawyer. The word *desiderata* means "things that are desired." Ehrmann wrote this work for himself, "because it counsels those virtues [he] felt most in need of." In my case, the following words were written on a poster, superimposed over a picture of a beach or sunset:

Go placidly amid the noise and the haste and remember what peace there may be in silence....

The first sentences hooked me. The voice struck me as that of a loving power, something bigger than I was. It offered impeccable advice in mysterious language. As I finished reading, a feeling of warmth and light washed over me.

I didn't realize it at the time, but this was my first spiritual experience, even if I happened to be surrounded by bongs and edible underwear. Clearly, God had a sense of humor.

I didn't buy the poster that day. I was with friends, and the Orange Julius kiosk was likely beckoning. I may have even forgotten about it, only to rediscover it again a few years later, then a few years after that. Yet it's fair to say that from that day forward, the Desiderata became my most reliable source of comfort and reflection. Clear and uplifting, the words—part poetry, part prose—felt timeless to me. They helped me every time I read them.

Here is the Desiderata, with some reflection from me:

Go placidly amid the noise and the haste and remember what peace there may be in silence.

There is a lot of noise and haste, and I like to think of its effect on us as akin to the fate of a frog in a pot of water gradually being brought to a boil. The frog may feel fine for a while, but soon, inevitably…it burns up. The same is true for people. It's likely that in the years to come, you will find yourselves falling victim to an endless onslaught of deadlines, scads of data, unsolicited opinions, and the whitewater of change for change's sake.

How is it possible to go placidly, as the Desiderata says, amid what feels like a shit show?

My motto is to keep it simple. To maximize success in chaotic settings, you must do this: Control how you appear to others as you regain your internal equilibrium.

While I agree that it's what is inside a person that is important, this is one situation where appearance matters a lot; the adage *Never let them see you sweat* is instructive. Everyone gets stressed, but with few exceptions, nobody really cares or wants to hear about your stress, much less see you sweating. Frenetic is a bad look. However frantic you may be feeling, it's important to never appear out of control. Instead, emulate the duck that appears to glide effortlessly along the water's surface with no evidence of exertion, keeping its vigorous paddling hidden from view. Mastering keeping your cool under stress is a key to developing "presence." (More on that later, but for now I'll just say that presence and leadership are often intertwined.)

If projecting calm feels unnatural, or phony, fall back on another old saying: *Fake it 'til you make it.* Being calm and steady in pressure situations is a crucial habit to cultivate.

Of course, this raises the topic of authenticity. Gaps between how you feel and what you do should always be examined and minimized. Anne Morrow Lindbergh put it this way: *The most exhausting thing in life is being insincere.*

So how do you align your roiling insides with a calm exterior demeanor?

There are an endless variety of self-care practices that can help you relax. Find one, two, or ten that work for you, but again, there's no need to overthink this. Calming yourself down can be as simple as remembering what peace there may be in silence.

What helps me is what I call my *daily discipline*—spending a quiet hour or so each morning getting centered, reviewing plans, and ensuring that key relationships are being well tended. If that feels like too much, it can also help to find a peaceful spot and do a quick breathing exercise. Here's one developed by Dr. Andrew Weil that I prescribed for my clients called 4-7-8 breathing. Inhale for four counts, hold for seven seconds, then exhale slowly for eight seconds. Do this a few times and your heart rate will drop, and you'll feel calmer. It's a great quick fix. I use it multiple times in a day. But don't let that be the only tool in your kit. I'll share others, later. For now, suffice it to say, keep calm and carry on!

As far as possible, without surrender, be on good terms with all persons.

There is a lot in this simple phrase, but first, I'll focus on the words *without surrender.*

You may wonder, "Without surrendering what?" My answer: your integrity, your core values, and yourself. Think of the adage *To thine own self be true.* You must know yourself first, which means knowing your values and principles.

I find values discernment difficult. My tendency is to like them all, rather than winnowing my list down to three or four core tenets. I'm a moral relativist, prone to injecting, "Yeah, but what if your child was dying, and..." hence ending up with a too-long list of values that provides no real guidance for me.

What helped me was to consciously figure out my own personal boundaries—the closely guarded principles that were worth taking a stand on, no matter what or who was involved. Looking back, my own personal lines in the sand ended up being justice for all, my children, and bullying. I try not to hate anyone, but I'll admit—I'm triggered by bullies. When I see violence or bullying behavior, my urge is to respond in kind. I'm pretty adept at moving past that impulse, though. Mean people suck, and my nature is to focus on more conciliatory results.

An example: When I was a young lawyer in private practice, I had a frequent adversary who was a complete asshole, many years my senior, and skilled at using his well-honed bullying tactics against my clients. He put the fear of God into them. Let's call him Ken. Because that's his name.

I tried every approach I could think of to make my interactions with Ken more positive, to inch closer to a win-win result for our clients. I could not surrender, though I was scared to death of him. The mere sound of his voice on my answering machine had my stomach in knots. But I had a client to represent and, sadly, with Ken on the other side of the table, to protect.

Ultimately, I knew I would have to heed the age-old advice from my dad about standing up to bullies no matter how uncomfortable. And in practice, carrying out this advice was lovely. We were at an early morning meeting, and Ken was in rare form, his nasty tone coupled with histrionics and threats that brought my client to the verge of tears. I stayed calm, which made him kick it up even more.

As he paused for a breath, I turned to my client and said, in a conversational tone, "Remember when I told you about this intimidation thing Ken does? This is it." I then turned to Ken and said, "We were wondering if this act of yours works every time or if being an asshole sometimes has a downside?" And then I was silent, eyes fixed on his. Silence is so powerful. Ken cleared his throat, shuffled some papers and listened as I outlined a few reasonable next steps. He then offered a wan smile and handshake before leaving, neutered. We managed to end things on good enough terms. But I did not surrender. And from that point forward, he was not a problem.

Speak your truth quietly and clearly...

The word *quietly,* here, means respectfully, devoid of excessive emotion or grandstanding. It's generally better to offer praise in public and criticize privately.

The word *clearly* has its plain meaning. The trouble is, in high-stakes conversations, being clear can feel difficult. But even more difficult, at least for me, is this axiom:

...and listen to others, even to the dull and the ignorant; they too have their story.

If listening is hard, listening to people who are less informed than you are can be downright maddening. Be extra careful that you don't judge or get short with these folks. It's easy to do. But remember, they've likely experienced dismissiveness many times before and hate it. At best they will think (and likely signal to others) that you're an elitist asshole. Being able to take a breath and move beyond our initial impulse to anger (or worse) and instead move toward compassion and empathy is what distinguishes humans from the rest of the creatures in nature. Or, as Robert Frost wrote: *Forgive my nonsense, as I also forgive the/nonsense of those that think they talk sense.*

Switching from fear to love can happen in an instant,[3] as it did during a fury-fueled town meeting I attended back September of

---

[3] The most powerful example of me turning on a dime toward love happened in 1979, when my first love told me that her mother, whom I adored, was a lesbian. I had made a comment disparaging gays and Jude picked that moment to tell me. Years earlier, a paper route customer tried to get in my pants, and not understanding that pedophilia was unrelated to sexual orientation, I conflated the two. In that instant, the scales fell from my eyes, and I actually felt lighter. Any remaining antipathy or judgment I felt about anyone's sexuality dissipated instantly.

1990. In my mind's eye, I can still see the young mother holding her baby with one arm, a toddler clutching her right hand, as she nervously approached the microphone set up in the middle of the Rescue Squad firehouse in Waterford, New York. The Village Board was holding a hearing on siting a boarding house for homeless people living with, and dying from, AIDS, and the crowd was standing-room-only. I was with Support Ministries for Persons with AIDS, the proponents of the project, and we were outnumbered at least 10-1. But what worried me most was the free-flowing bar in the back and the Dutch courage the alcohol was giving to a bunch of men who were becoming increasingly vocal and crude as the night wore on, eventually driving away the moderator from the League of Women Voters. The communal adrenaline was palpable, and I was seething inside, having spent hours listening to the dull and ignorant screaming of village attendees who didn't want a bunch of "queers/fags/junkies/degenerates, who would infect them and maybe even diddle their children.

Then, the mom stepped to the microphone and, using more polite language, spoke haltingly about her opposition. As tears streamed down her cheeks, she wondered aloud how she could ever care for her family if she and her kids "caught AIDS."

It was impossible to not feel compassion for this woman who, while terribly misinformed and acting out of fear, was, in her heart, just doing what comes naturally to parents. She was trying to protect her kids.

I stood there, listening intently, my heart rate dropping and my moral certitude giving way to a slowly dawning realization that there was more than one right way to accomplish our goal. While a rigorous public education campaign might not bring the men at the bar over to our side, we clearly needed to look at why our existing efforts to educate people on the science of HIV contagion were failing to produce better results. So we brought in doctors and nurses cloaked in lab coats and scrubs to disseminate their subject matter expertise. No polling was done, but we were able to ratchet down the vitriolic response over the next few months.[4]

Avoid loud and aggressive persons; they are vexatious to the spirit.

Oh, yes, they are, and some of these people know it and use it

---

[4] The AIDS Boarding House project was a real eye-opener for me in other ways, too. As chair of the site selection committee, I was bound to encounter NIMBY-ism regardless of where we looked to site the project. What I soon discovered was that outside groups were applying equal pressure from the other direction. The founder of ACT-UP Albany, the Rev. Dan Ritchie, happened to be on our board. Dan Ritchie was a firebrand who learned at the knee of the movement's founder, Larry Kramer. There was, at the time, little positive about the relationship between ACT-UP and the Democratic machine that had dominated Albany for nearly 100 years.

I didn't want to get caught in the middle of these two powerhouses, so I persuaded Dan to let me set up a meeting with one of the deans of Albany politics and a former judge, John Holt-Harris. I knew he was a good man, if a bit insistent that things be done in an orderly fashion. To me, this meant no surprises. I sold Holt-Harris on taking the meeting as a means to getting briefed on our plans. Dan didn't need any coaching. While he was capable of doing dramatic things to raise AIDS awareness, he also knew when to don his clerical collar and be the Right Reverend! And he knew as well as I did that it was worth at least one meeting to ask for the support of the state's power structure.

When we arrived at Holt-Harris' office, we noticed that the chairs opposite his desk were actually well-appointed Shaker rocking chairs, and as we sat, Dan and I shared a hopeful look that the rest of the meeting would be as comfortable. I don't remember the details, though I do recall that Holt-Harris listened and asked good questions. We apparently had good answers because—and this I remember clearly—at one point he stated that our project had "significant merit," spun around, grabbed his phone and speed dialed the Mayor of Albany, Tom Whalen. Fifteen minutes later, Dan and I were in the Mayor's office reviewing possible locations with his director of planning. While we ultimately chose a site just outside of Albany, we were able to establish a relationship with the Machine, and a productive conversation began. Don't let uneasiness with another party fool you into thinking that a trusted partnership is impossible. You can always ask!

...

as a weapon. Like Ken. In his book *The No Asshole Rule,* author Robert I. Sutton writes about the toxicity of certified assholes whose bad behavior is ingrained in their character. These are people who interrupt others, violate personal space, and on and on.

Life is too short to put up with assholes. Plus, Sutton notes, being an asshole is highly contagious. Simply being around angry and aggressive people noticeably alters your mood and behavior for the worse.

See also, *This too shall pass.*

If you compare yourself with others, you may become vain or bitter, for always there will be greater and lesser persons than yourself.

To stop comparing, it helps to be able to distinguish between symbols of wealth and true success. The status symbols, it turns out, are fleeting; dead ends. As a child, I wasn't overly covetous or envious of what my friends had, and my parents weren't concerned about keeping up with the Joneses. Still, there were class rankings, test scores, box scores—lots of opportunities to compare myself or my team to others.

True success is generated from within you. It may be invisible to others, but it leads to fulfillment and inner peace. We all know the importance of looking inward for self-esteem, especially at a time when it has never been easier for extrinsic factors like social media to make us feel less-than.

In your early teens, you guys survived a few episodes of mean girls, false accusations, and bullying. Anne, I still remember when you had just started middle school and your mother and I decided to be responsible parents and spy on how things were going on social media. At first, we were aghast to read that several of your closest friends from grade school were ganging up on you. It was eye-opening to come face-to-face with how mean those girls could be.

But when we read your responses, we were heartened. You pushed back against bullshit each and every time, you were truthful and more pleasant than the circumstances required, and you would not be moved off what you knew was right. So, while our snooping initially filled us with a sickening feeling, in the end, we felt greatly encouraged. We knew you were strong and resilient and capable of handling whatever life threw your way. Boy, were we right on that count. Consistent with both sides of our family, you are very fair but suffer fools almost never.

Jack, I'm not going recount details here; details fade, feelings endure. But I do recall a time when you were falsely accused of something that could have had serious consequences. I can't begin to express how proud I am of the way you handled things. You told the truth calmly so many times to different inquisitors, plus you were able to compartmentalize over a weeks-long ordeal so other aspects of your life didn't suffer. (See above: *Never let them see you sweat.*) You have made your mom's and my job easy. The investigator later told me that he wished the complainant had your clarity of mind and grasp of the relevant facts.

But if you ever find yourself being bullied, in an unexpected jam, or feeling afraid, here are some suggestions you may find useful:

- Pause and take a breath. Absent having a gun to your head, or being in imminent danger, clearing your head so you can make a thoughtful plan is the first step.
- Figure out whether the fear is legit before planning. F.E.A.R is almost always an acronym for "false evidence appearing real." It's a trick our brain plays to keep us safe, even when no physical danger lurks.
- Consider the "audience"—in this case, any other people involved—and try to ascertain what their goals are and what they are uneasy about.

- Assess how much information you have and how you can fill in your knowledge gaps. That often means finding people to advise you. The ultimate goal: to get everyone on the same page about the truth.
- Figure out how to manage your information risk, meaning who can know what. Your advisors are your innermost circle. Outside that group, be careful what you share.
- Assume good intentions of others until you are shown otherwise.

Jack, in your case, we were executing our plan to seek a win-win solution, until I discovered that the other guy was determined that it was his way or the highway. Ultimately, it was your interview with the investigating officer that carried the day. I was so proud when he told me what a good young man you were. Those are the moments that parents live for.

This process of defeating the bullies at hand all happened naturally because I simply applied the same techniques I used at work. Law school probably helped a little, but it mostly came down to the advice in this book.

Enjoy your achievements as well as your plans.

This desideratum resonated most for me. I LOVED to make plans and was fond of saying, "Let someone else hang the drapes." This was fine later in my career, when I had people to whom I could delegate. Early on, though, I had to make a mindful pivot toward executing plans myself.

Until I did, I would forever buy books and not read them, buy equipment for a new hobby and not engage, etc. Along the way, I noticed that my tally of unexecuted plans correlated with the length of time I'd neglected my daily discipline.

Eventually, I realized that all my unfinished business was a sign that my life was unbalanced and that I was awarding myself a trophy for simply having a good-looking plan.

Sometimes, the problem was in my approach to planning. It's important, I learned, to always begin projects with the end in mind. Your objective must be crystal clear, whether you are writing an appellate brief, leading a team project, or planning a family vacation. If you don't do this from the outset, the fuzziness of your goal will eventually become apparent, and the costs in extra time and resources can be steep.

Keep interested in your own career, however humble; it is a real possession in the changing fortunes of time.

Stephen Covey would call this suggestion—to keep interested— "sharpening the saw." A human resources person might refer to this as career development. What it comes down to is investing in yourself. Take a class that makes you better at your job. Get certified in something that will make it difficult for the company to let you go in a down time.

The best example of this in my own career was taking a master's level course in strategic planning at SUNY's School of Public Health. In my job at the American Cancer Society, we were proposing to build the Manhattan Hope Lodge, a no-cost, 60-room temporary living facility for out-of-town cancer patients who traveled to New York City for treatment. As Project Manager, I knew it would require our leadership to make an eight-figure financial commitment that was significantly beyond their comfort zone. I would have to get them used to a new comfort level, and in my semester-long class, I learned, among other things, the process of making this happen, as well as the importance of ensuring the numbers were right and the timeline accurate. The project was completed on time, and at budget. By doing my due diligence, I made myself into the consultant I would have otherwise hired, and it was fun.

Exercise caution in your business affairs, for the world is full of trickery. But let this not blind you to what virtue there is; many persons strive for high ideals, and everywhere life is full of heroism.

Among my too-pronounced character traits is a fear of failure (thanks, Mom!), which includes the sometimes-odious desire to please others. Yet funnily enough, these traits worked to my advantage when it came to sussing out "trickery" in business. I was rarely duped.

This is mainly because in my professional life, I was never averse to asking accomplished people for help. Later, I'll go into the importance of relationships and what truly motivates others, but for now, all you need to know is that my willingness to ask for help became a big upside for me.

A good example of this occurred when I was in law school. After my second year, I attended an awards banquet with my classmates, including all the Law Review members and faculty. I hadn't made Law Review due to my atrocious first semester (I'd been overconfident in my intellect; previously, it had allowed me to skate a bit. Hubris, really.)

And while I was a finalist or semifinalist in the big criminal and appellate contests, I hadn't taken top prize in any of them. I could stay in the background that night, spending the evening relaxing as I watched higher-ranked students haul in prizes. Or so I thought.

To fully appreciate what happened next, you should know that when I was around 10 years old, I attended a huge YMCA banquet and with no warning was called up to receive a big sportsmanship award. My photograph and name landed in the Schenectady Gazette. From that day forward, I would sit at big events and compose bits of an acceptance speech in case I ended up at the podium. I know. Such an ego. Except I did no such mental composing at the law school banquet because, as noted above, I had zero expectation of winning anything.

What I didn't know was that the final and most coveted award, for Best Advocate, was about to be awarded to...me. And they expected me to say a few words. By the end of my remarks as, ahem, Best Advocate, I had the whole place rolling with laughter—because of my incomprehensible acceptance speech. Not a single memorable line, probably due to the absence of any complete sentences.

Among those laughing loudest about this blatant incongruity between the award I had won and the quality of my speaking was the most distinguished professor of law, not just at Albany Law School, but throughout the state of New York. David D. Siegel came up to me afterward and told me that he found my remarks genuine and unpretentious. The next time I saw him in school, he again mentioned that he found what I said to be charming and memorable.

Emboldened by this, I asked Professor Siegel to be my thesis advisor. Although he had never served as such, he agreed. My motive in aligning with him was that I knew, with his mentorship, I could get my final paper published in the Bar Journal. And I did. Not quite the same as making Law Review, but darn close.

The lesson for you two could be as simple as recognizing and surrounding yourself with good people. And I'm sure you will. But this desideratum also invites us to consider virtue, high ideals, and heroism more broadly. In this case, virtue and high ideals enabled me to move beyond the disappointment of not being on Law Review (and thereby missing out on the more lucrative job offers) and find a way to move forward.

Be yourself. Especially do not feign affection. Neither be cynical about love; for in the face of all aridity and disenchantment, it is as perennial as the grass.

We have so many faces, so many relationships, and so many places where we work and play. Add to that the fact that we live in an ever-changing world, where we are constantly evolving, and it's downright miraculous that any of us could ever claim self-knowledge. But it's possible, and it's necessary. As my mother liked to put it: Nobody likes a phony baloney.

While none of us can or should remain static, it's crucial to be true to your inner core. It goes back to knowing who you really are—what your core values are. It's what's inside that endures and matters.

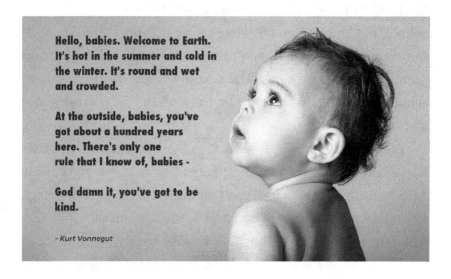

Hello, babies. Welcome to Earth. It's hot in the summer and cold in the winter. It's round and wet and crowded.

At the outside, babies, you've got about a hundred years here. There's only one rule that I know of, babies -

God damn it, you've got to be kind.

- Kurt Vonnegut

You are probably sick and tired of this humblebrag (or flex); I've told this story too many times. But I'm going to tell it one more time. Last time, I promise!

At every parent-teacher conference, I would have two questions for your teachers. *Were you kind to others generally? How did you engage with the classmates who were on the social periphery, who might have been picked on or ostracized?* Perhaps because I was a slightly older dad, I knew that if you were able to read and write, the only thing left to pave the way to true happiness was being kind and empathic. And while I'm not going to presuppose what those values are for each of you, I know you are both very kind people.

Take kindly the counsel of the years, gracefully surrendering the things of youth.

To me, this means that you should never try to look or act younger than you are. You do you first, but don't try too hard. You'll figure it out.

It does remind me of how many times we went grocery shopping, Anne, and you kept trying to get me to buy a bottle of Just for Men to dye my hair. My God, how you got a kick out of that!

Nurture strength of spirit to shield you in sudden misfortune. But do not distress yourself with dark imaginings. Many fears are born of fatigue and loneliness.

My strength of spirit was sourced from the unfailing belief, which I talk more about later, that *this too shall pass.* I always knew that whatever bad times I was experiencing, things would get better.

You may wonder how I can say that with this goddamn disease. But the truth is, some days are far brighter than others. And the dark imaginings—my God, I could choose to take the pain of this diagnosis, hold on to it, and feed it until I had created within myself an unbearable, needless suffering. My buddy Mike, with whom I drank a lot of coffee, cleverly noted that he had a built-in "awfulizer." He said there was no situation that his mind couldn't make catastrophic in an instant. This was my customized mental awfulizer!

To break free, every day, I try to put the yardstick behind me and revel in the abundant joy in my 58 years rather than mourning the impending loss. Nobody gets out alive. And I've been given the gift of advance warning.

This is a super-hard attitude to maintain, so sometimes I must choose to restart my day. Life, like baseball, is a game of adjustments, right, Jackie?

A word on fatigue and loneliness.

For many years, I visited church basements with others and heard lots of pithy sayings that fit on placards. But one was a keeper, and that is the acronym *HALT,* which stands for hungry, angry, lonely, tired.

HALT was meant to serve as a reminder to ask yourself whether any of those adjectives fit when you happened to be feeling shitty. If I realized I was angry, for instance, maybe I'd take a walk. One of my buddies had a saying: *Move a muscle, change a thought.* I also found that moving my body pretty much guaranteed a new perspective. Part of it is simply because of time elapsing (i.e., *this too shall pass*), but it's also the case that even a little exercise changes up your brain chemistry. So, you end up feeling differently whether you want to or not. It's the same as when you dread going to the gym but are invariably glad you did.

Interestingly, I find the same concept works with loneliness. When you're lonely, it's hard to reach out and connect with someone. (Use Zoom and texting as a last resort.) Ask someone to meet you for coffee or at least have an honest-to-God conversation by phone.

I found an elegant solution to dealing with mental fatigue and the awfulizing that often followed. In law school it was common for me to read, write, and study for 10 hours at a stretch. My solution to the fatigue was to master the 12-minute nap. Every hour or so I'd set the alarm on my watch (no smartphones then) and treat myself to rejuvenation. After about a month I didn't need the alarm anymore, and to this day I can catch 1 to 40 winks, as needed.

Go forth and master this habit and feel how refreshing it is. I brought the napping habit to the law firm, and it blew the minds of the other young associates to see me sleeping on the job. The partner supervising me asked if it was true that I periodically napped in my office. I said it was but asked him to consider the news through the lens of productivity. He smiled, wagged a finger at me, and said he was wondering what my secret was. Fun moment, but it never caught on as a firm-wide practice.

Beyond a wholesome discipline, be gentle with yourself.

The adage *Moderation in everything, including moderation,* is on point here. Yes! By all means, practice habits that make you more effective, but don't be a slave to them.

It's much more effective to put energy toward your physical, mental, and social health—your overall state of well-being—than it is to try to pinpoint and alter every single negative behavior. Physical, mental, and social health are also closely connected, and focusing on all of them is the best, most holistic form of self-care. For instance, if you neglect your skills and knowledge, you may get fired from your job, which might lead to your feeling like a victim and blaming others. This would affect your social relationships, leading to stress, which would compromise your physical health.

A holistic approach to self-care is the best defense against burnout and the negative chain reaction that neglecting one area can bring about.

Ehrmann brings it home with these lofty, but true, final desiderata. I found great comfort in his imagery:

You are a child of the universe no less than the trees and the stars; you have a right to be here. And whether it is clear to you, no doubt the universe is unfolding as it should.

Therefore, be at peace with God, whatever you conceive it to be. And whatever your labors and aspirations, in the noisy confusion of life, keep peace in your soul.

With all its sham, drudgery and broken dreams, it is still a beautiful world.

Be cheerful. Strive to be happy.

CHAPTER 3

Build a Strong Foundation

The Desiderata counsels that beyond cultivating wholesome discipline, it's also important to be gentle with yourself. If you set the performance bar too high, then continually fall short, you may start beating yourself up. If that happens repeatedly, you can create a negative cycle of falling short.

So how do you cultivate a gentle yet effective daily discipline? For me, it was a process of trial and error. I was never able to carve out a rigorous daily routine in stone, but over time I managed to amass a toolbox of reliable practices to help me meet whatever challenges I was dealing with at full strength.[5] Still, even with all the variability, I can safely call the tools in this section my essentials.

---

[5] My best self-management teachers were the writings of Benjamin Franklin and Stephen Covey. I recommend Walter Isaacson's biography of Franklin, and Covey's *7 Habits of Highly Successful People.* I do have to say that after whatever project I was working on was complete, I would invariably become bored with the routine I'd created to help me work, and let it go. I might come up with a new routine for

➤ My Daily Discipline

Ideally, good habits begin as soon as you awaken. The problem for me is that, like you, Anne, I love the quiet of staying up late, then happily sleeping in until I wake up. Now that I am retired, I've mainly reverted to that routine, but as I began writing this book in earnest, I realized that I needed more energy and productive time, so I reached for my toolbox and changed things up. The first step toward making a change is recognizing that a change is needed.

During my first few jobs in my 20s, my morning routine was...trying to get to work on time. I had no plan. There was no breakfast—the most important meal of the day!—because I either didn't have the time or felt jittery and rushed. Usually, I had stayed up or out too late the night before, which didn't help.

By the time I got to my desk, got caffeinated, had a few stop-and-chats, then finally turned my attention to work, it was usually after 10 AM, meaning that I'd passed at least four unproductive hours. For the rest of the day, I'd inevitably feel as if I was playing catch-up. And seeing colleagues already buzzing about productively when I was just getting into gear made my imposter syndrome even worse.[6]

---

the next challenge, or else just sit loosely in the saddle until circumstances called for a bespoke fix.

[6] Around this time, my universe became better aligned. First, there was Covey's implicit remonstration about my lack of a spiritual life. Then my weed-addled fiancée showed some shockingly poor judgment, and our ill-conceived engagement ended. There I was, 28 years old, single, with sole possession of a downtown brownstone and three quarters of a life plan written.

That's when I decided that en route to finding my as-yet-undefined spiritual life, I would clean up another item that had been bugging me.

Women.

After a string of disappointments, I felt I had a blind spot in this area, a faulty picker. Feeling bold, I went to see the free counselor offered through work. Over time, this counselor helped me immeasurably, but when I suggested during the very first visit that my choosing the wrong women was at the root of my issues, she

In Chapter 2, I refer to my epiphany about needing to develop a spiritual life and the steps I took in that direction. This was also the time when I was introduced to journaling. I started my mornings by brewing coffee, reading a short, inspirational passage from a meditation book, and then writing.[7] That reading, reflecting, and writing exercise is what I call my sometimes-daily discipline. It's a tool I've used intermittently, and when I do, I start my day in a positive (as opposed to a frenetic) frame of mind. I really encourage you to adopt this, or an equivalent practice, every day.

I do have a caveat to add: If you only ever journal on what's missing in your life or what's going wrong rather than also reflecting on what you do have, you'll end up snuffing out the feelings of gratitude this exercise can elicit. So try to be balanced in your journaling. With some practice, you can focus on the completeness of the present moment—the positive as well as the negative. To help me avoid a purely negative mindset, I rely on several mantras: *This experience is complete, just as it is.* And, *I am complete just as I am.* These can help to keep your mind away from thoughts about what's missing so you can focus on what's important.

In time, I built out my journaling routine to include a plan for each workday, where I listed and prioritized tasks for the day in my planner, along with unfinished tasks from previous days. As a result, I felt less stressed in the mornings and clear about what I needed to accomplish.

---

nearly bit a hole in her lip to keep from laughing. She wanted me in a basement, post haste. I resisted at first, but ultimately relented and found the missing spiritual dimension in my life. Giving up drinking and drugs was easy. What I had was a thinking problem.

[7] I did my writing with a typewriter given to me by my dad. He gave the most thoughtful gifts. Dad never asked what I wanted; he somehow just knew. It was one of his many hidden talents that I didn't recognize at the time. He was such a great guy.

My routine changed, however, when I went to law school. It was more laid-back than work life, and I relished the less structured schedule. What a mistake that was! I told myself that I was still getting my work done, or so I thought. Unlike most jobs however, in law school, you only get feedback once every four months. At the time, my most important class was Torts, a four-credit course. I felt confident enough about that class, since I was an active participant. I reasoned that I would at least get a *B*.

So, when Professor Moore posted the grades on her office door, the *D* I saw there felt like a punch in the gut. I walked away, stunned, then later approached her office nervously, as if for the first time. No luck. Still a fucking *D* in Torts.

In hindsight, I think I caught a break with that grade. I was hung up on getting good marks so that I could make Law Review, and along the way, I lost perspective on why I applied to law school in the first place.[8] My legal writing teacher, Linda Fitts, bought me a copy of Dr. Seuss's *The Sneetches,* which reminds us that the happiness that flows from external things and accomplishments tends to fade. Lasting satisfaction is an inside job. I had heard and read that before, but I had not yet learned that happiness was also an inside job. While chasing a spot on Law Review, I had been acting like the covetous Sneetch who pursued the elusive star only

---

[8] I went to law school in part because I felt I had pissed away my undergraduate years. I thought about business school, but through my search for a spiritual life, I got involved in an AIDS advocacy group (referenced earlier) that sought to establish the nation's first boarding house for people living with the disease. The upstate New York community where we wanted to locate the shelter fought back so hard that we sought redress, successfully, in federal court: *Support Ministries v. Village of Waterford, NY,* 808 F.Supp 120 (NDNY 1992). I was at the epicenter of that case, having found the location in dispute and also the law firm that represented us pro bono. All of which directed me toward a career in law. The clincher was when John Holt-Harris spun around in his chair and got the Mayor to see us right away. That move was flat-out sexy. I wanted that kind of influence!

to clamor for its removal when it fell out of style. I didn't really want to be on Law Review; I wanted the accomplishment of making Law Review. My desire wasn't authentic.[9]

As it turned out, second semester classes were even tougher than the first. And if I didn't improve dramatically, I was in danger of flunking out. Then I recalled having seen another truism Scotch-taped to nicotine-stained walls in church basements. It read:

If nothing changes, nothing changes.

What then, was I to change? It wasn't obvious. I finished my reading assignments, went to class, and paid attention. That was more than I had done in college! After reviewing my final with Professor Moore, I realized that while I had read the words in my books, I didn't understand what they meant or portended at a deep enough level. As I began looking closer at the order of my days, hoping to find a silver bullet that would help me turn things around, I noticed I did all my reading at night. And then I remembered a Ben Franklin habit I had overlooked—*the magic three hours*—and proceeded to implement it.

By simply going to bed at a decent hour, I was able to get up at least two hours earlier each morning—at 5 AM instead of 7 AM. This was a real game changer for me. I discovered that I could accomplish nearly an entire day's work between 5 AM and 8 AM. Ben Franklin also said that there was "gold in the mouth of the early morning hours." And I'm happy to say I found it. I became a

---

[9] My friend, Mick Florio, introduced me to the teachings of Syd Banks, who described his epiphany as beginning when a complete stranger told him, "You're not insecure, you just think you are."

Speaking of complete strangers, remember our oceanside lunch when we went to Cardinals spring training, Jackie, after my ALS diagnosis? Remember the old man who randomly stopped at our table and advised us to treasure every moment? We were twins in our amazement! I hope someday you'll tell your kids that story. It still gives me goosebumps.

star constitutional law and contracts student and scored nearly a 4.0 that second semester. My law career was safe.

This experience taught me that when deep comprehension of complex subjects is required, it's best to get to it in the morning, and this has held true throughout my career. I can't say I have maintained this discipline on a daily basis, though I often wonder what I might have accomplished if I had. In any event, whenever I feel up against it, I pull that tool out of my box and use it for as long as it takes to get myself on track.

Of course, I realize that using early morning hours this way is not a panacea, and it's not for everyone. So, go ahead and find your own sweet spot for working. I'll just leave it with the thought that there's a good chance you're not putting the dawn hours to their best use.

> CHAPTER 4

Adopt Critical Thinking as Your Operating System

C ritical thinking is a (gently) disciplined approach to evaluating information and reaching conclusions based on evidence. One crucial thing to remember: You have to be open-minded to think critically. When you are biased in favor of a particular outcome, you can run into trouble. Today, with the advent of fake news as well as increased polarization, especially along political lines,

it's easy to wonder if critical thinking even exists anymore or is valued. It is. I can confidently tell you that few skills are as valued by employers. Why? Because anyone who regularly practices critical thinking invariably makes better decisions. The chart on the preceding page illustrates the point.

Critical thinking is such a powerful preparation tool that it often reveals knowledge gaps you didn't know existed. In law school, for instance, I was taught not only to prepare my cases, but to prepare the other side's cases as well. While this took a little extra time, it inevitably showed me the true strength of my position and, for the most part, eliminated potentially fatal surprises in court. I also learned that if I outprepared my adversaries using this method, I won more often, which meant happier clients. And happy clients don't bitch as much when they get their bill.

Think of it this way: There is stuff you know and stuff you are aware you don't know (but will try to learn). What's most dangerous of all, however, is the stuff you don't even realize you don't know. It's tough to come up with a good defense when someone presents information you didn't realize existed.

Here's another example: When I was a private-practice lawyer, I was often hired to conduct investigations of alleged wrongdoing by public officials or government employees. I was gaining a reputation as the go-to guy for cases where, as my adversaries would say, the person under investigation had done nothing wrong. This characterization stung a little. My adversaries were often union lawyers, and I believe strongly in collective bargaining.[10] But the truth is that I also loved investigating because I could usually detach from an outcome and enjoy the pursuit of the truth. Facts were what they were, and I found that if I dug a little deeper to find evidence of wrongdoing, I was able to earn my fee, albeit in a way that I hope was evenhanded.

---

[10] It turned out that the most satisfying thing about getting my Actors Equity card was being able to crow about being a union guy in a Labor Day Facebook post.

I recall one case where the accuser was a person of supposed great integrity who had recently been recognized for being the best in her profession. While the governing body of this institution hired me to investigate, it was she (the accuser) who provided me with a road map for my work. Because she was immensely credible and strongly backed by the governing body, I followed her lead for a while. Yet two months of intensive and expensive investigation yielded scant evidence. I felt wobbly.

It was then that I realized my mistake: I had forgotten to think critically. I walked the law firm's senior partner through my work and reminded him that our confidence in this investigation was, at the outset, grounded in the stellar reputation of this decorated public official and that we needed to go back and question our assumptions about her credibility. He agreed. Very soon after, I discovered that our star witness was, as they say in Texas, all hat, no cattle. Her infallibility as a witness fell apart quickly, and we ended up able to move forward and investigate the accuser.

After recovering from their initial shock, the governing body accepted my report and my recommendation that they remove this person from office.

You needn't go to law school to master critical thinking. When you encounter new information or are beginning any project, the following questions will help you discern what you know from what you don't; what you have and what you still need.[11] I've also found these questions helpful in having

---

[11] The foundational imperative for problem solving is to define precisely what the problem is; far too often, people successfully solve the wrong problem. The example that has stayed with me for years involves a hotel that wanted to replace its elevators. Management had received numerous customer complaints about slow elevators, and their experts opined that the elevators couldn't be adjusted to go faster; they needed to be replaced at a cost of over $4 million. Luckily for the hotel, someone

productive conversations with people who lack information, or those who live in a bubble and get their news only from one or two biased sources.

While there is no one set of questions that work for every situation that calls for critical thinking, you can't go wrong if you test your assumptions, ask stakeholders lots of open-ended questions, and follow the money. Below, you'll find some good questions to start with that will ensure you are doing the necessary critical thinking.

First, ask who...
...benefits from this?

...is this harmful to?

...makes decisions about this?

...is most directly affected?

...are the key people to discuss this with?

Next, ask what...
...are the strengths/weaknesses of this idea?

...might another perspective be?

...would be a good counterargument?

...is the best-/worst-case scenario?

...is most/least important about this?

---

brought in a human factors expert who told them that their problem was not slow elevators. The more precise challenge was that too many customers perceived that the lifts were slow. The consultant recommended that the hotel install mirrors on each floor by the elevator bays. When the hotel did, at a cost of $40,000, the complaints stopped. It turned out that customers didn't mind waiting if they had something pleasurable to do, like looking at themselves. The moral of this story is that there is no assumption that should not be questioned when homing in on the problem you are trying to solve.

Then ask where...

...have you noticed similar concepts or situations?

...is there the most need for this?

...in the world would this be a problem?

...can you get more information?

...do you go for help with this?

Ask when...

...will this benefit our society/company?

...would this cause a problem?

...is the best time to take action?

...can you expect this to change?

...should you ask for help on this?

Then ask why...

...is this a problem/challenge?

...is it relevant to me/others?

...this is the best/worst scenario?

...has it been this way for so long?

...has this been allowed to happen?

...is there a need for this today?

Finally, ask how...

...does this disrupt things?

...do you know the truth about this?

...will you approach this safely?

...will you see this in the future?

This is a good place for me to recommend getting a proper mentor. You will doubtless learn from many people in all of your jobs, but I suggest you find space in your life for at least two trusted advisers: one who works where you work, and another mentor outside of work with whom you can develop a mutually satisfying, longer-term relationship. I received and adopted this advice early in my career, and it has been enormously valuable, even more so than I can elaborate on here.[12] (For more on how to choose a mentor, go to Appendix B.)

---

[12] By the same token, I'm a big fan of sometimes bringing my work/career-related thinking or issues to a therapist or counselor, if I'm seeing one at the time.

> CHAPTER 5

Apologize Gracefully

"The weak can never apologize. Seeking
forgiveness is the attribute of the strong."
—*Gandhi*

When you have hurt someone unnecessarily, or have made a mistake, you need to make an authentic apology. An authentic apology shows your regret and acknowledges, without excuse, that your actions, intentional or not, have hurt others. If delivered with grace and sincerity, such an apology—which I outline below—is the most effective way to restore trust in a strained relationship.

Another benefit of a genuine apology is that it can open a dialogue between you and the other person. Your willingness to acknowledge your misstep gives the other person the chance to give voice to his feelings, even if those feelings include anger or other emotions that are hard to hear. It can also open up a constructive dialogue about your relationship as a whole and help you avoid a similar situation in the future. After a well-executed apology, you'll often notice that you feel a sense of relief; truly, it's one of the best ways to restore your integrity in the eyes of others.

Think of it this way: If you don't apologize when an apology is warranted, you risk damaging your relationships with colleagues, clients, friends, or family. This can harm your reputation and earn you an "asshole badge," particularly if you aren't apologizing due to arrogance or self-righteousness. It can also limit your career opportunities and lower your effectiveness—besides which, others may not want to work with you or engage with you on any level. And when you become a boss, your failure to admit your mistakes can create a toxic work environment, causing hemorrhaging of talent and productivity.

So, what does a good apology look like, as opposed to a lame one?

1. *Say the words.* Start by saying "I'm sorry" or "I apologize." This signals to the other that your remorse is front and center, which makes it safe for them to listen instead of mentally preparing for battle. But be sure you're being authentic and clear about why you want to apologize. No ulterior motives and no qualifying language.

2. *Don't dilly-dally.* Apologize as soon as you realize you've wronged someone.

3. *Admit responsibility.* One way of doing this is to remind yourself to avoid using the word "if," as in, "I'm sorry if you were offended…" or "I'm sorry if I upset you." We've all heard these non-apologies, and the word *if* is the tell. Stay away from that word when apologizing; it implies you don't think you did anything wrong, and that you're subtly shifting the blame onto the other person, which negates your apology. When I am on the receiving end of one of these apologies, I reject it out of hand by restating the

apology properly and asking them if that was what they intended to say. It's a bit aggressive, I admit, but conditional apologies are one sign that you might be dealing with an asshole.

I have to say that over my lifetime, I've noticed that the quality and sincerity of people's apologies have gotten progressively worse.[13] To my mind, they've become conditional and crafted to (not so) subtly blame the recipient as a snowflake—a person who is too easily offended.

If you think the other is partly at fault, your apology is not the time to address this. You are there to focus on your actions, over which you have control. Clean up your side of the street and don't risk turning amends into an argument. Empathize. Put yourself in that person's shoes and imagine how she felt.

4. *Make things right if you can.* You'll want to think carefully about this step, because a token gesture or empty promise will do more harm than good. The flip side of this is important as well: Because you feel guilty, you might also be tempted to give more than what's appropriate—so be proportionate in what you offer.

This is a natural corollary to a psychological phenomenon known as *reciprocity,* which I will cover in more detail later. For now, understand that humans find it uncomfortable being in someone's debt and will often offer something of greater value than

---

[13] Apropos of nothing, I've noticed a similar erosion of standards for whether or not to give a standing ovation at the end of a performance. I recall taking a bow after a poor performance of a shit play, and the audience got on their feet. It made me feel even worse. Don't succumb to peer pressure. If a show is worthy, your legs will know. Otherwise, polite clapping will suffice.

what they have received to get themselves out from under that sense of obligation. This dynamic is deeply rooted in the social contract, and usually, it will work to your advantage, whatever side you are on. When the debt you owe is less objective, however, it can be tough to know what will help square things up, especially when you care about the relationship and feel bad; that's when you're prone to offering too much. What has helped me in these situations is to ask the offended party what, if anything, I can do to make things right. (Incidentally, this is also a great time to turn to your favorite mentor to check your thinking.)

5. *Emphasize the importance of the relationship, offer a solution and explain how you'll avoid repeating the action or behavior.* By doing this, you reassure the other person that you won't make the same mistake again. This helps rebuild trust and repair the relationship. Make sure, however, that you honor this commitment in the days or weeks to come. If you promise to change your behavior but don't follow through, others will question your reputation and your trustworthiness.

More apology tips:

- Be fair to yourself when you apologize. Take full responsibility only for your part.
- Don't expect forgiveness on the spot. Give the other person time to respond without rushing them.
- If you're apologizing on behalf of your organization, get advice from your boss or a legal professional first.
- The nature of the apology should really follow the offense. So, if the offense given was public, the apology should be public, and vice versa. In contrast, if you had a private argument with a friend, you should take them aside and apologize privately.

- Don't apologize when you've done nothing wrong. Excessive apologizing diminishes your credibility and authority.

So, given the pronounced effects, why do some people still refuse to apologize?

The truth is that apologies are hard. It takes courage to put yourself in a vulnerable position, to possibly open yourself up to attack or blame. Some people struggle to show this courage or surmount their own self-centeredness.

Take me, for example. You guys have been kind about reassuring me that I've been a good dad, but I know you will both agree that among my least attractive character traits is my impatience.

It will not surprise you to know that you are not the first to have told me that I was impatient or too quick to raise my voice. Whenever I heard that criticism, I had to fight the urge to argue back with a tsunami of justification and self-righteousness. In my mind, I was not only right, but others also needed to change their behavior!

I was wrong to think that.

Whatever my protestations, my behavior demonstrated concern for myself, not others. To paraphrase the founding list-maker, selfishness and self-centeredness! That, I think, was the root of my troubles. So, I'm going to follow my own advice, and take a last pass at a sincere apology.

To you, Anne and Jack, Sally, and all my family, loved ones, and friends: I want you all to know that I really regret every time I was short-tempered or impatient with you.[14] I realize that my actions

---

[14] I also know that, at times, my impatience spilled over into asshole territory. I was once at a breakout session at a conference where the facilitator had us follow each other through a labyrinth. It was about being contemplative and becoming centered. When it ended, the facilitator asked me what I thought about while walking the labyrinth. I told him I was thinking that the guy in front of me should hurry the

were hurtful and squandered time that we could have enjoyed. Jack and Anne, you deserved a better example from your father. Sally, you deserved better from your husband in so many respects. I hope you will forgive my shortcomings. I don't know what I can do to demonstrate my conviction at this point except to acknowledge my contrition publicly. What I can say is that I haven't had relationships that have mattered more to me, and it was my loss that I didn't treat them with greater care. You guys are beautiful people.[15]

Jack, this apology brings to mind something that happened when you were about five years old. We were at the dinner table, sitting glumly, because I had just been cross about something. Afterward, when I offered an apology doubtless blanketed in justification, you earnestly asked a question that is central to why I am writing this book:

"Dad," you said, "how do we get that time back?"

Of course, the answer is, we can't. Those moments are gone.

Please. If you take anything away from this book, it is this: Try to remember that every moment matters.

---

fuck up. Which was true. When we were walking, the guy in front of me was really into it and walked very, um, prayerfully, like he was in Machu Picchu, or wherever the fuck. The poor facilitator looked so crestfallen. I should have kept my mouth shut, or just snuck out.

[15] "The most beautiful people we have known are those who have known defeat, known suffering, known struggle, known loss, and have found their way out of the depths. These persons have an appreciation, a sensitivity, and an understanding of life that fills them with compassion, gentleness, and a deep loving concern. Beautiful people do not just happen." – Elizabeth Kubler-Ross

> CHAPTER 6

Forgive Generously

"Always forgive your enemies.
Nothing annoys them so much."
—*Oscar Wilde*

When I was in my late 20s, I learned that if someone wronged me, it was entirely my choice whether to hold on to resentment and the (occasional) vengeful thought —or to forgive and get on with my life. Or, as my friend Larry liked to say, let go or be dragged.

Truth be told, I used to get dragged a lot. Not anymore.

Forgiveness isn't something to be done for others. It's something to do for yourself. Because not forgiving someone is the equivalent of staying trapped in a jail cell of bitterness, serving time for someone else's crime.

Of course, feeling resentful and holding on to grudges is a universal experience.[16] The causes, however, are multifarious:

---

[16] Resentment can also arise from careless remarks. I'm reminded that you can tell you're at an Irish family reunion if it begins with a drink, turns at some point to singing, and ends with someone uttering the words, "And just what is that supposed to mean?!"

Maybe you've got your back up over a critical (or impatient) parent, or someone who hurt you but won't accept responsibility; or you can't forgive a spouse who has been unfaithful. Whatever the cause, psychological and wellness research suggests that forgiving will improve your physical, emotional, and spiritual well-being, and that hanging on to resentment has the opposite effect.

According to the Mayo Clinic, forgiving and letting go of grudges can lead to...

- Healthier relationships
- Improved mental health
- Less anxiety, stress, and hostility
- Lower blood pressure
- Fewer symptoms of depression
- A stronger immune system
- Improved heart health
- Improved self-esteem

If you don't forgive, you could...

- Bring anger and bitterness into every relationship and new experience
- Become so wrapped up in the wrong that you can't enjoy the present
- Become depressed or anxious
- Feel that your life lacks meaning or purpose, or that you're at odds with your spiritual beliefs
- Lose valuable and enriching connectedness with others

Another practical benefit of forgiveness is that it reduces the amount of time I've wasted ruminating about my offense, reimagining what I should have said or done differently, or worse, being pulled to the dark side and envisioning vengeance. But there is a greater upside still.

Life is just a series of moments. If you allow resentment to really take root in your mind, you're handing your offender a degree of control over your life. Given that all of us have so little control in the first place, we can't afford to give any away. The point of forgiveness is to focus on reclaiming your peace of mind and the space in your brain that your offender has been occupying.

One more point: If you are lucky enough to be forgiven, it doesn't mean that what happened was OK, and it won't necessarily mean you will be welcome in the life of the person you've offended. Forgiveness just means that the person is done carrying around the pain.

The reality is bad things happen. Shit breaks and people let you down. In life, some pain is inevitable. However, the suffering that comes with holding on to resentments past their sell-by date is optional. You've probably heard that before but knowing something intellectually is one thing; really understanding it in your heart is another. The foot-long journey from my head to my heart can sometimes seem like an impossibly long distance. How, then, can you get the words *I forgive you* to resonate in your heart?

My own epiphany came during the time your uncle was robbing banks to support his heroin addiction. I knew he was in rough shape, but I had no idea how rough. When we offered him a place to stay, he managed to clean out our bank account, so I gave him the boot. He promised to work off the debt, but of course that never happened. His fall from federal prosecutor to junkie was complete.

Then, in November of 2005, an acquaintance told me to look at the Schenectady Police Department website and see if I recognized the man featured on their home page. Son of a bitch. It was your uncle Andrew, and he was on the lam. For days, I had been seething over how he had stolen from us; now this. I perseverated about all the shoes yet to drop: the inevitable arrest,[17] the rampant publicity, the impact on our aging parents, and, selfishly, the imaginary humiliation and stain on our family's reputation.

That was the backdrop for the insight I had a couple of weeks later. After his arrest and the front-page news on Thanksgiving Day, it seemed that everyone I ran into wanted the scoop on my brother. Without much thought, I spouted out my gloom-and-doom take on what had happened. Whether I wanted sympathy, or I really believed my little brother was a hopeless cause, I don't know. But after retelling the story a couple dozen times, I heard the voice of Dylan Thomas saying, "Somebody's boring me. I think it is me."

I simply couldn't bear to tell the same sordid story again. That's when it occurred to me that I had the choice to answer people's questions with a message of hope and possible redemption without blowing smoke up anybody's ass.[18] I realized then that I was the boss of my story. Rather than tell a tale about how fucked he was, I talked about his resilience and his focus on putting this behind him and getting his life together. It wasn't a Pollyanna story. I acknowledged that it would be a difficult for him to rebuild trust and that time would tell, but I was optimistic, and his family was behind him.

---

[17] I found out that he was wanted by police ten days before his arrest, and I agonized over whether to turn him in. I asked my two mentors for input. One rightly pointed out that hundreds in the area would recognize him and turn him in if I didn't. Further, they felt as if my taking action would only make our already wobbly family dynamics worse. I finally rested my decision to not act on the fact that none of the news stories that mentioned your uncle referenced a gun. I promised myself if that changed, I would have to reconsider.

[18] Sure enough, he did his five-year bid in the klink, got released, and wrote this: *Sheer Madness: From Federal Prosecutor to Federal Prisoner, a Memoir by Andrew McKenna* (2014). I'm proud of him. He knows the monkey is off his back, though the circus is still in town. Andrew's second book is due sometime in 2020. He's got this.

So, yes, I told a different, hope-filled version of the story that was just as true as the "he's fucked" story. I immediately felt better by telling the recovery version. My heart was lighter, and it was easier to take your uncle's apology to heart, to forgive him, and to begin the reconciliation process.

When I visited Andrew in the county lockup, he apologized and expressed remorse during what ended up being six or so conversations. It was easy to forgive him. Telling a new story enabled me to do this authentically and also increased my capacity for compassion.

> CHAPTER 7

How to Have a Difficult Conversation

When I was jammed up at work, I could often trace my troubles to a difficult conversation that I was either not having or that I was trying to have but that was not going well.

What is a difficult conversation? To me, it's characterized by high stakes, strong emotions, and opposing points of view. Ironically, the more important the conversation, the higher the risk that we fail in communicating our message, because emotions and our reptilian, fight-flight-freeze brain tend to take over. Thus, in conflict situations, where being human is most important, we are prone to act like animals.

To reach a good resolution and avoid putting more stress on a possibly already frayed relationship, it's crucial for each person to bring an open mind to the discussion and to be transparent— not always easy to do. I believe there are two ways to make a conversation safe: We must care about the other person's interests and goals, and they must know we care.

One reason we often hesitate to fully engage in a difficult conversation is that we feel unsafe, sometimes because of the stories we tell ourselves about the character and objectives of the person on the other side. But remember that our emotions come from made-up stories we tell ourselves, not from reality and facts. And it's easy to become emotional during difficult conversations, leading us to assume that the other person has the worst possible intentions, which escalates emotions.

To break this negative pattern, you need to look at all other possible stories and change your judgments and conclusions. A great way to do this is to get curious. Ask yourself: "Why would a reasonable person like X act and behave like this? What belief brought them here? What if I treat them in accordance with that belief?" By expanding the breadth of the story you are telling yourself about the other person, you will come to any difficult conversation feeling calmer and better prepared.

It's also important that you take a close look at your own role in the relationship. How have you contributed to the problem? What are your objectives for yourself, for the other person, and for the relationship? Be honest with yourself: If your goal is to win an argument or make yourself look good, that's an unacceptable objective. Dig deeper. Consider questions like "How can I do X and still do Y?" or "How can I do X and not hurt Y?"

Another consideration: When it comes to important but difficult conversations, we are likely to feel wobbly and less confident in our message, and so we water down our objectives and end up not saying what we want to say. That's why it helps to start difficult conversations with facts. The tone will be less personal, you'll be more credible, and you're more likely to stay on message. I also particularly like the idea of starting from a point on which you both agree, so you can begin on a positive note. Continue developing mutual options based on points of agreement wherever possible, then move on to the points of difference.

The authors of *Crucial Conversations* offer the acronym STATE to help break through the emotions and conflicting objectives that can get in the way of mutually satisfying resolutions.

S = Share the facts
T = Tell your story
A = Ask for the other's story
T = Talk tentatively
E = Encourage testing

Keep in mind, too, that understanding each other and fostering a positive tone are not the end goals. They are the means to an end, which is finding a mutually acceptable solution. Once you do, I recommend keeping a record of any decisions that have been made, and who is responsible for what.

➢ CHAPTER 8

On Your Journey, Rely on These True Things

Hopefully, you'll make the steps I outline below part of a gentle daily discipline so you can gain the maximum benefit. But even if you don't, I highly recommend adopting at least this first thing:

Learn to regain mindfulness quickly. Once you do, it is always available to you at any moment and can be particularly helpful when you need to regain your objectivity, or when it's crucial to communicate well with others. Most people are broadly aware of the concept of mindfulness, which is everywhere these days, but that doesn't mean they have a mindfulness habit. Some find it mysterious or have no idea how to start; others are dismissive because the whole idea of mindfulness feels weird. My best advice for you when it comes to mindfulness, again, is to not overthink this.

Simply put, a mindful state is characterized by the calm, objective, and somewhat detached feeling you get during and after fully concentrating on yourself, your body, and your breathing. It doesn't have to take long to achieve this state, and no chanting is required.

Start by being still and listening to your own mind and body. This can be as simple as sitting down and concentrating on your breathing. Focus completely on the moment, not on the past or the future. Just concentrate on you, your health, and your emotional state in the moment. If that feels like too much, it can help to find a peaceful spot and do a quick breathing exercise like the one I described earlier—the 4-7-8 breathing.

And if all else fails, take a nap. Doing so allowed me to read and study alertly for hours at a time.

➢ Evict the Committee in Your Head

Sometimes, I'm convinced there is a small, windowless conference room in my head, one with wobbly chairs and a broken thermostat. It's usually unoccupied, but occasionally, especially when I feel out of balance, the room silently fills up with nine nasty old men, probably representing the circles of hell. All of them carry binders full of proof that I'm fucked. Whatever the issue, the consensus is always the same. *Fucked.*

The insidious part is that these purveyors of doom are actually me. I listen to their bullshit and believe what they say—that I'm not up to the task, that I'm an impostor and that disaster is imminent.

It's easy to forget that these nine nasty men are in my mind—that they're not separate beings. And so, I allow them to continue to occupy rent-free space in my head. I forget that thoughts precede and dictate our feelings. I do this despite the fact that it leads to a miserable downward spiral. There are endless ways that this committee can convince me that I'm useless—and they can do it at warp speed.

Yet as real as they seem, my thoughts and feelings are and always will be ephemeral; they do not define who I am. So, to fight back, I need to resist falling into autopilot mode where I mistake my thoughts and feelings for reality. It just so happens that I have a good tool for that, which some New Age gurus describe as "watching the thinker."

To use it, you first need to be aware that you're in a bad spot; that you've fallen into the ever-present trap of believing you are what you think and feel. Gaining this awareness can be the hardest part. When I first started using this tool, it took a while—sometimes days, weeks, even months—to realize that I had slipped into a bad spot and needed to adjust my perspective. Usually, the best tell that I was out of kilter was what I called "hamster head." This typically occurred at night when I was trying to sleep. Like a hamster running faster and faster on an exercise wheel, I would be consumed by an endless cycle of doom-and-gloom thoughts, caught in an endless loop of frustration and angst.

Today, I'm able to recognize those mental funks more quickly. When I do, I can self-correct in minutes by applying one of my most effective tools: I walk into the metaphorical conference room and evict the entire peanut gallery. It may sound crazy, but this adjustment is a powerful way to regain perspective because the true me is separate, capable, and loved, despite what the committee may say. And it is possible to own your thoughts and feelings rather than the other way around.

Here's how the tool works: First, I take a figurative step back and observe the committee in my mind. To cement the fact that I am separate from my thoughts and feelings, I listen to their criticism and quiz them about their proof, much like a cross-examination. I might say, "Oh, look, you're back again," or, "These crotchety old men are making shit up again. Plus, they're trespassing." Then I calmly evict them. Actually, the eviction is pretty profane. Who am I kidding?

While this may seem like a silly exercise, it interrupts the negative thoughts and breaks the relentless downward spiral of time-wasting worry and regret. My hope is that you learn to quickly recognize when you feel aversion or fear, or when you are lost in a fog of self-denigration. Then you can remind yourselves that these feelings, as always, are impermanent and will pass.

By the way, this phenomenon can also work in reverse. The ego revels in transforming any good thing that happens into an inflated sense of self-worth, which can set you up for wildly inaccurate expectations that the high will continue. The truth, sad as it is, is the good times do not last forever.

If you fall for the ego's trick, you will assuredly plunge from the greater height of inflated expectations, which results in greater hurt. To avoid this pain, remember that just as the tough moments pass and yield to new thoughts and feelings, so, too, will the good moments yield to something new. As the investment commercials warn, past performance is no guarantee of future results.

➤ All You Have Is the Present Moment

*"When people are not in the moment, they're
not there to know that they're not there."*
—*Ellen Langer*

One thing I've discovered over my life is that the mind—and not external circumstances—is responsible for our emotional pain or upset. And it's the mind that can prevent you from living in the present, which can keep you from being happy.

How does the mind accomplish this trick? By recalling memories of the past, or by projecting into the future. What's important for you to know is this: If you let it, your brain is capable of filling your entire existence with regretful memories and anxiety-ridden future scenarios.

Most of us act as if we have power over the past and future, even if we know better. It's as if we're programmed to forget that we can't alter what has already happened nor predict what will happen. Instead, we perseverate over things beyond our control, which reminds us of our powerlessness and creates still greater pain.

I've found that the best way to free yourself from pain is to observe the mind without judgment, which helps you separate yourself from your thoughts.

Start by internalizing this fact: *Your thoughts, and the feelings that result from them, are not the authentic you.* To put it another way, the authentic you is not what you think and feel.

For example, craving an apple is different from consciously noticing, "Oh, look—I'm having thoughts about craving an apple now." With the former, your craving becomes sneakily synonymous with who you are, and the thought becomes your identity, which we know is untrue. In contrast, the latter observation simply states a fact. And when you phrase a thought this way—as an objective thought—you heighten your ability to become an acute observer of your own mind, detach yourself from your thoughts, and distinguish between your mind and your authentic self.

The more you practice this technique, the easier it will be to gain some separation from your thinking.

Begin by simply noticing your thoughts and impulses without judging them, labeling them, or acting on them. Ask yourself: "What am I thinking about now? How are these thoughts influencing me?" What you'll start to discover is that shifting your perspective this way—from becoming your thoughts and feelings to simply observing them—will remind you that these thoughts and feelings aren't actually you, which can help ease suffering.

Watching my thoughts come and go reminds me (for the gazillionth time) that my thoughts and feelings aren't really me. Usually, that's enough to end any suffering I'm going through.

Of course, not all pain is avoidable. As you and I know, sorrowful things do happen in life. Sometimes, they catch us unawares, before we've even had a chance to worry. Other times, something we've long been afraid of ends up coming to pass.

That was the case with my ALS diagnosis. While on a business trip in November 2017, I went to the gym and found I couldn't budge a 20-pound dumbbell with my left arm. This was strange because I'd been curling more weight just a week before. Then I remembered that in October, when moving some furniture with my roommate, my left hand kept slipping off what I was carrying. I also couldn't explain the rampant fasciculations (muscle twitches) that were happening in my arms and chest. Nobody believed it, but I knew in my gut what was the matter.

Over a two-week period that wrapped around New Year's 2018, I went to three different doctors and asked them point-blank: *Do I have Lou Gehrig's disease?*

The first doctor said she really didn't think so, but she called in a favor to get me a neurology exam because she didn't like what she saw. Just days later, the neurologist uncovered more symptoms and told me it was 50-50. He was an interesting guy. He suggested I look on the bright side—that Stephen Hawking had lived for a long time. Then he ordered a special scan to rule out a spinal tumor and said that was the best I could hope for. It was December 28, 2017.

"Holy shit," I thought, even managing a grim smile while

awaiting a cab to the train ride back to New York City, thinking my father would have liked this doctor's candor. I recall really wishing my dad were still alive. I could have used a talk.

A week or so later, I heard the words I had most feared hearing since I watched *The Pride of the Yankees* with my dad when I was maybe 10 years old:

You have ALS.

After getting the news, I walked out of the Eleanor and Lou Gehrig ALS Center and onto West 168th Street feeling completely numb. I lit a stress cigarette and walked to Coogan's, an Irish pub a couple blocks away. I got home to Astoria but only have spotty memories of the next few hours. On the A train back to midtown, I made a futile attempt to jot down a to-do list, then stopped. I can't even remember what I put on the list. I was too shaky for list-making.

Instead, I took out my phone and Googled another list: Elisabeth Kübler-Ross's five stages of grief: denial, anger, bargaining, depression, and, finally, acceptance. I couldn't place what stage I was in. I needed a "none of the above" option. Maybe I was just in shock.

You may be wondering how I coped, and if I used any of the advice I'm sharing in this book. In my mind, I can hear Jesse Pinkman from *Breaking Bad* shouting, "YO!! How did all that 'stay in the moment' shit work when you heard that news, yo!?"

The short answer is that I did use these tools, haphazardly and unintentionally, perhaps, and I don't know what I would have done without them. But given the certainty of my own death in the foreseeable future, I'll admit that staying in the moment became difficult. All I could think was that I was abandoning you guys.

When I got back to my apartment that day, I grabbed my journal and started what I guess you could call writing, though when I read those entries months later, as I was packing to move out west, I found them both indecipherable and horrifying, so I threw them away. Shortly after that, I lost my ability to write, type, or text, so there is no written record of my experience except for what I've written here—my recollection of that time from a two-year distance, written with eye-gaze technology.

I can't claim to remember everything, but I did earn a passing grade on the Desiderata maxim *Nurture strength of spirit to shield you in times of misfortune.* I say that because I don't recall making any conscious decisions to help limit my pain. Instead, I seemed to automatically turn to the strategies I always used, like journaling, doing breathing exercises, napping to keep up my energy, and asking for help and accommodations when I needed them. Like muscle memory, practicing with these tools all along had helped me to develop at least a modicum of a strong spirit.

I also bought a whiteboard and filled it with affirmations, then pretended to believe them: Gehrig's *I feel like the luckiest man on the face of the earth* and *I've got a lot to live for* quotes along with a paraphrase of the Jane Kenyon poem "Otherwise": *Someday, it will be otherwise... But not today.* I would meditate on these phrases, among others, two or three times a day. I guess you could call it fake-it-'til-you-make-it mode.

I also tried to take control of the things I could, like making sure to check off bucket-list travel destinations and adventures. Jack—your suggestion that the two of us go to see the Cardinals' spring training was brilliant.

I also kept working for as long as I could because we needed the money, it kept my mind occupied, and because I didn't want to stop. I loved my coaching job, and oddly, the quality of my insights improved. For the next six months, I think I was a better coach. It's possible that having zero fucks left to give left me with a new perspective.

Listen: I'm feeling a little glib as I write this, so let me not forget to mention the many times since my diagnosis that I've broken down into the most awful jags of ugly crying.

Fast-forward to the present and a worldwide Covid-19 pandemic.

Annie: I took to heart the challenge posed in your epic Facebook essay—to hold up the pandemic and my diagnosis, two situations beyond my control, and use them as a mirror that could reveal something about me that needed tending.

I didn't experience an immediate epiphany; the reveal was gradual. I took a couple weeks off from writing. This hiatus proved up a quote by Lao Tsu that I first heard in a long-ago lunchtime visit to a church basement: "Muddy waters let stand, will clear."

When my own muddy waters cleared, I took inventory and realized my (sometimes) daily discipline had gone missing. So, I took a mental step back and observed my thinking, which was unfocused. In fact, it made me dizzy.

I realized that the committee in my head had been reconstituted. Instead of sabotaging me, they were planning a pity party. One little fucker wrote my obituary. I tore up his draft, cancelled the party, kicked the whole damn committee out, and instead composed this gratitude list:

1. My wife, Libby, is an extraordinary caregiver and I love her to pieces. I want for nothing.
2. I don't have to worry about my job (I don't have one).
3. I've got plenty of the liquid food that gets pumped into me.
4. We've got bidets, so toilet paper is not an issue.
5. My loved ones are safe and, thus far, healthy.

With the benefit of a clear head, I saw that the pandemic and my eyes getting wonky notwithstanding, I needed to get a wiggle on. My physical capabilities were not going to improve, and this book was not going to write itself.

So yes, the tools worked, alleviating my suffering more than any treatment my amazing doctors could administer. My life went on, as your lives will go on when I die, probably right around the time this book lands in your hands. And you may wonder what you can do to avoid excess suffering on top of the inevitable pain you will experience.

The best I can suggest beyond using the tools in this book is to accept the situation for what it is. That means knowing you'll mourn and feel sad—that's a given. When you lose a loved one, feeling sad is natural, so you don't need to feel guilty or ashamed about it.

But—and here's the crucial difference—if you can accept the sadness as something you feel NOW and remind yourself that eventually your feelings will change (sometimes several times a day), you will be on the right track. And if you're able to avoid layering regrets or resentment on top of sadness or mourning, that's even better. Thank goodness we at least had time, huh?

So here it is again, for posterity: In my last days, nothing makes me happier than knowing that each of us did the work in front of us, for ourselves and each other. We bloomed where we were planted, and all is as right as a world with this cussed disease can be! Well done, us!

Living in the present provides you with the inner strength to accept difficult and painful facts of life. It does not, however, require you to live a passive life or to be a pushover. Inner peace is not worth much if your outer life is a shit show, so remember that it's always possible to manage your actions and change things within your control.

There are also times where it's natural and even imperative to focus on the past or future—but in a constructive way, to extract lessons from your experiences and plan for what's to come.

A simple example is the need for a postmortem or debrief after you've finished a project. This is especially important when you're working on a team where you and your colleagues can benefit from hearing multiple experiences and perspectives.

I favor a debriefing process used in the U.S. Army known as an After-Action Review (AAR), a good example of when and how to use the present moment to consider the past. Specifically, an AAR is a quick and reliable way to extract the lessons, both good and bad, from any experience and to improve the next time. The classic AAR involves a short meeting, often held standing up to emphasize that it's meant to keep things on track and discourage people from going off on tangents. The goal is to tightly focus on what happened, why it happened, what was learned, and what adjustments need to be made going forward, without recriminations or blame.

For that reason, it's important that everyone "check their rank" (or, in most cases, job title) at the door. This allows leaders and team members to get the unvarnished truth. (A leader, especially, needs to avoid the danger of others telling her what they think she wants to hear.)

In other words, to get the most out of an AAR, everyone needs to approach it dispassionately, treat the lessons as data, and move on.

➤ This Too Shall Pass

"Let everything happen to you. Beauty and terror.
Just keep going, no feeling is final."
—*Rainer Maria Rilke*

Despite everything I've talked about so far, you'll likely find yourself chewing up time worrying about the future. We all do. Our reptilian brain and egos are on good terms with the nine-man committee I talked about earlier. And while this team is indeed practiced in making us miserable, they eventually bend the knee before the following perfect truth, one I've already used several times in these pages: *This too shall pass.*

Rather than try to describe the obvious, read this oft-cited story to get a sense of how taking on that state of mind can help:

There lived an old farmer who had worked in his fields for many, many years. One day, his horse bolted away. His neighbors dropped in to commiserate with him. "What awful luck," they tut-tutted sympathetically, to which the farmer only replied, "We'll see."

Next morning, to everyone's surprise, the horse returned, bringing with it three other wild horses. "How amazing is that!" they exclaimed in excitement. The old man replied, "We'll see."

A day later, the farmer's son tried to mount one of the wild horses. He was thrown on the ground and broke his leg. Once more, the neighbors came by to express their sympathies for this stroke of bad luck. "We'll see," said the farmer politely.

The next day, the village had some visitors—military officers who had come with the purpose of drafting young men into the army. They passed over the farmer's son, thanks to his broken leg. The neighbors patted the farmer on his back—how lucky he was to not have his son join the army! "We'll see," was all the farmer said!

So, when pain takes over your mind and you start projecting a state of endless gloom, remember the desideratum that cautions against "dark imaginings" and use the tools I've been talking about.

And when you're thinking about the future in a more positive way—that is, savoring the anticipation of good times to come—it's also smart to exercise some caution. Remember that your ego would love nothing more than to leap from the present moment to prematurely celebrate success that hasn't happened yet. Hold off. The best planning for the future will happen when your mind is clear and you are fully present.

> CHAPTER 9

Everyone Is Massively Self-Interested

"Nobody cares how much you know until
they know how much you care."
—*Theodore Roosevelt*

If someone shows you a group photo you are in, who do you look at first?

It is perhaps unfortunate but definitely true that we are all massively self-interested. You will often hear businesspeople, especially those in sales, ask, "What's the WIIFM"—an acronym for *What's in it for me?* In my experience, I've never seen someone make a decision or take action unless they believed it was in their own interest to do so. That makes evolutionary sense: We are motivated to do what helps us survive and thrive. Even the most charitable, giving people are motivated by self-interest; their self-interest just happens to be different. But they still act in ways that feel personally beneficial, just like the rest of us overtly selfish bastards.

Rather than bemoaning the "social repugnance" of this fact, as David Foster Wallace put it (see below), it makes more sense to internalize it, because it happens to be fundamental to success and happiness, in life and in business.

First, though, I'd like to go back to Wallace, who balefully acknowledged this self-centered worldview in his masterful commencement speech at Kenyon College in 2005.

> *Everything in my own immediate experience supports my deep belief that I am the absolute center of the universe; the realest, most vivid and important person in existence. We rarely think about this sort of natural, basic self-centeredness because it's so socially repulsive. But it's pretty much the same for all of us. It is our default setting, hard-wired into our boards at birth. Think about it: there is no experience you have had that you are not the absolute center of. The world as you experience it is there in front of YOU or behind YOU, to the left or right of YOU, on YOUR TV or YOUR monitor. And so on.*

> *[...]*

> *It's a matter of my choosing to do the work of somehow altering or getting free of my natural, hard-wired default setting which is to be deeply and literally self-centered and to see and interpret everything through this lens of self. People who can adjust their natural default setting this way are often described as being "well-adjusted," which I suggest to you is not an accidental term.*

[...]

Look, if I choose to think this way [...] fine. Lots of us do. Except thinking this way tends to be so easy and automatic that it doesn't have to be a choice. It is my natural default setting. It's the automatic way that I experience the boring, frustrating, crowded parts of adult life when I'm operating on the automatic, unconscious belief that I am the center of the world, and that my immediate needs and feelings are what should determine the world's priorities.

Which is to say that if you are trying to persuade someone, you need to check your own self-centeredness at the door and make it about them. To do that, you need to use language and address topics that make clear what the benefit is to the client/person/whoever you happen to be dealing with.[19]

Back in the mid-1960s, Professor Warren Wittreich did foundational research on factors that maximized client engagement. He examined the topics professional services salespeople led with during client meetings and grouped them into two buckets: client-focused topics that were very much intrinsic to the client, and topics that were extrinsic—typically about the seller, his products, or his firm.

Guess which set of topics was vastly preferred by clients and resulted in more productive meetings, not to mention more sales?

Yet most of us, even salespeople, are more comfortable talking about ourselves and what we have to offer. Why? Because we've practiced talking about these topics all of our lives, and we are in control of the narrative and therefore less likely to be challenged.

---

[19] I use "client" as a catch-all for whomever you are sitting across from. It could be a boss, colleague, prospective customer, spouse, or child.

Even salespeople who swear they are talking about benefits intrinsic to their customers are typically wrong. This stems from a fundamental misunderstanding of what a benefit is, as opposed to a "feature" or an "advantage."

Here's an example to help you distinguish among features, advantages, and benefits whenever you are trying to convince someone of something.

- **Feature** (what is it?): I've got a big umbrella (so what?)
- **Advantage** (what does it mean?): It easily covers two people (so what?)
- **Benefit** (why is it important?): You and I can walk to the meeting without getting wet

Often, we are so close to the features and advantages of whatever it is we are talking about that we assume the client can figure out the benefit to themselves on their own—that it's obvious. But failing to make the benefit explicit up front is a big mistake. You don't want to leave the logical leap from feature to benefit up to your customer, because you don't want to make them do any work. For one thing, attention spans are tiny and getting tinier. And for all you know, the client might be running on two hours of sleep and no lunch and has just gotten reamed out by his boss.

So always explain the benefit to your client first. People buy into benefits and also the people who deliver them. Not sure if you are speaking in benefit language? As in the example above, ask yourself "So what?" (from the client's perspective) again and again, and you'll end up with the benefit. Lead with that.

If it is of interest to your client, they may ask how that benefit is delivered. That's when you talk about features and advantages, explaining the feature (what it is) and the advantage (what it means).

➢ CHAPTER 10

The Fear Factor

"Everyone feels blame more acutely than praise."
—Charles Darwin

I believe all human actions fundamentally spring from either love or fear. I also imagine that love will ultimately prevail. But being fully human means acknowledging the degree to which fear, and our pronounced desire to avoid discomfort, impact our decisions and actions.

➢ Overcoming Fear to Become an Expert Networker

I happen to be an introvert (my Myers-Briggs type is INTJ, in case you're wondering), and it took me a long time to feel comfortable with big gatherings or events that had no purpose other than meeting new people. Of course, I didn't actually hate meeting people; I just thought I hated meeting people. And when the event had a work overlay (the despised networking event) where it was expected you'd be attending to drum up business—well, then I felt acute discomfort. It felt like every person magically transformed into a bag of money, which I found awkward and unnatural. God, I hated those things.

This is an example of what fear-based self-centeredness will get you.

I had it backward. For me, the right perspective for networking events was that I was there to meet and learn about interesting people, while keeping my focus skewed toward people who could help me advance my business. I brought, as my Templar Advisors colleague Gareth Lewis calls it, a *giving mindset,* where I thought about how I might be able to help people I met and whether there was something I could give, freely, with no expectation of anything in return.

Gareth would emphasize the importance of being genuinely curious, in addition to approaching with a giving heart. Ask good questions about the other person and you are bound to learn something new, in addition to achieving the always-helpful goal of talking less than half the time. Your questions shouldn't sound like an interview. The model to replicate is how you talk with your friends: fluidly, organically. We have things in common with our friends, and this often becomes the glue that sticks us together.

Your job in networking is to not hang around with your coworkers (bosses hate that), but to overcome your trepidation and discover the "glue" that will connect you to the people you meet along the way.

➢ Be Aware of Other People's Fears

It's crucial that you remember that fear is a powerful motivator. In the wrong hands, it can be used manipulatively. My goal here is the opposite: I offer the following advice to help you help others. Don't miss this point. Once you understand this, you will be more persuasive and, at the same time, helpful to others.

My former colleague, Templar director Charlie Garnett, once told me that all things being equal, a client will always award the sale to the person or company who best understands the client's pain and uncertainty.

This has been confirmed by ample science, and by my own experience.

Recall the importance of using benefit language when trying to persuade people (So what? WIIFM?)? We tend to think of benefits as good things (the root of benefit, *bene*, means *good*). But we mustn't forget that helping someone avoid an actual or potential downside is also a benefit. In their groundbreaking research, Daniel Kahneman and Amos Tversky proved that people feel the pain of a loss more acutely than they enjoy gains—we are more upset about losing $10 than we are happy about finding $10.[20] This means that how we frame the benefit matters.

Loss aversion is at work in all facets of our lives, not just when material things are at risk. This is why the bad feelings we have after getting a bollocking from our boss are exponentially more intense than the good feelings we experience after a positive meeting. It's reflexive: We expend more mental energy on setbacks than we do on progress.

---

[20] Incidentally, being rich doesn't help. For rich people, the pain of losing their fortune exceeds the positive emotional gain of getting additional wealth. My work with financial advisors to ultra-high-net-worth individuals confirmed this. Because they have so much (and, therefore, so much to lose), the rich often feel more vulnerable and anxious about the prospect of losing than someone living paycheck to paycheck. Is this rational? No. But it's how they feel.

Loss aversion

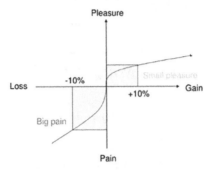

Roughly speaking, losses hurt about twice as much as gains make you feel good. So, if you can frame the benefit you bring as a potential downside that you can help your client avoid, your message may have twice the impact. But as with all benefit statements, you have to say the words; you cannot leave it to the client to figure out. I call this being helpfully explicit. You don't want to be a purveyor of doom, nor do you want to appear manipulative.

BENEFITS	positioned as AVOIDING DOWNSIDE
Building a mother-in-law apartment will increase the value of your property.	Moving your mother-in-law in will alleviate worry, guilt and the need for monthly trips.
This new model senses other cars in your blind spot, reducing the chance of accident.	Add the words: Has your 16-year daughter started driving yet?

You want the client to feel as if you've moved around the table to sit next to them, sleeves rolled up, ready to work on matters of interest to them—not that you're trying to make a sale. If a benefit of what you propose helps your client avoid a threat, find a way to discuss that candidly. Uncertainty is another fear-based feeling. Sometimes we can articulate why we feel uncertain or uneasy; other times it's a sensation in the gut. Either way, it deserves exploration. I have found that when we feel uncertain in a given situation, there are typically a couple of options. If the reason for the uncertainty is known, you can talk about it and try to resolve the discomfort. If you can't articulate why you're uncertain, give it some time. Remember: Muddy waters let stand, will clear.

Try to put off making a decision if your gut says *uh-oh*. Get in the habit of trusting your intuition. Rarely do we miss out by giving ourselves time to gain clarity.

To understand uncertainty on an interpersonal level, it's good to practice empathy—to put yourself in the shoes of the other. This is also a concrete step that can help you become a more empathic listener.

If you are trying to persuade someone to take an action, it's up to you to identify your client's uncertainties, teasing them out with genuine questions ("A number of my clients identify XXX as a concern. What are your thoughts on this?"). Once the concern is on the table, you must manage down the client's anxiety. Often, a conversation with the other person may resolve their discomfort, but it has to be the right conversation.

To prepare, you will benefit greatly from an exercise developed by Charlie Garnett. Take a sheet of paper and draw a line down the middle. On the left side, list all the benefits to your client for taking the action you propose. Be sure the benefits answer the questions *So what?* and *WIIFM?*

On the right, list all the uncertainties the other person may have. How will you know what they feel uncertain about? Hopefully, you've asked them directly. ("Given what we've discussed, I'd be interested in hearing from you about any concerns or uncertainty you have.") Write down all these potential uncertainties.

If you have pitched this idea to others (like a salesperson might), you can also mine those experiences and reactions. What objections have you heard in the past? What are the reasons others have given when they say no to your proposal? Put all of those on the list.

And of course, put yourself in the other person's shoes. Then, given what you know or have learned about them, list any other uncertainties on the right side of the page. An example:

OBJECTIVE : To convince this person to change financial advisors and hire me and my firm

BENEFITS	CLIENT UNCERTAINTIES
Our proprietary software platform enables you to see changes in your portfolio on a minute-to-minute basis.	While my present firm/software platform has under-performed, I like my current guy.
Our administrative team is highly experienced and can make the transition painless for you.	I hear that changing firms requires a lot of paperwork, and I am very busy. None of my friends invest with you.
We assign a team of analysts tailored to your investment objectives.	I'm not sure how my spouse will feel about this. The fees for single stock trade are too high.
Our senior portfolio manager is available to meet with you on a quarterly basis to answer any questions you have.	You seem very young to be an advisor.

I cannot overemphasize the value of this exercise in preparing for an important meeting or sales pitch. All planning for the meeting flows from this practice.

First, listing out the benefits and potential uncertainties gives you a menu from which you'll determine the key points you'll make. Most times you'll be pulling from the benefits side, but sometimes you'll want to preempt an objection by addressing an uncertainty (potential objection) proactively.

You likely won't cover everything on your list, and that's a good thing. Cover just the key points, and don't go beyond four of those (two or three is optimal). You also don't want to try to show all your cards and knowledge up front. You want to get questions, to encourage a two-way dialogue. Not only do clients prefer that, but a well-answered question helps you establish credibility while making the client feel good about having asked something smart.

Which leads me to the other value of this exercise. You (and your team) must be prepared with strong answers for all of the possible uncertainties/objections. If you prepare properly by predicting these, you put yourself in the best position for success.

> CHAPTER 11

Conscious Competence

"Be yourself. Everyone else is taken."
—Oscar Wilde

*"Wise men speak because they have something to
say; fools because they have to say something."*
—Plato

It's a bit broad, but if I were to bumper-sticker this lesson, it
would read: *Pay Attention!*

But that's too general. What I really want is for you to not
be on autopilot in certain high-leverage stages of preparing for,
and executing, important meetings. Another way to think about
autopilot is something called *unconscious competence.* When a
baby is born, they can't tie their shoes, and they aren't even aware
that's a skill they need to have. That is unconscious incompetence.
When they get a bit older, they become aware that they need the
skill, but lack it and still need help. Then they are *consciously
incompetent.*

When they do become skilled, however, especially the first few times, watch how they are totally focused on the task in front of them, being intentional to ensure success. That's called *conscious competence.*

Eventually, though, they have shoe-tying on autopilot and can succeed with little to no conscious thought. That's *unconscious competence.* Operating on an unconscious competence level is fine for many things, but when getting a good result is important, it's good to reexamine those bits where we've gone on autopilot and regain our conscious competence.

Even if we've had thousands of meetings, we will always do better if we can revert to a consciously competent level in preparing certain high-leverage parts of the meeting or conversation. It needn't take long, but it is axiomatic that we get better results when we've got a plan.

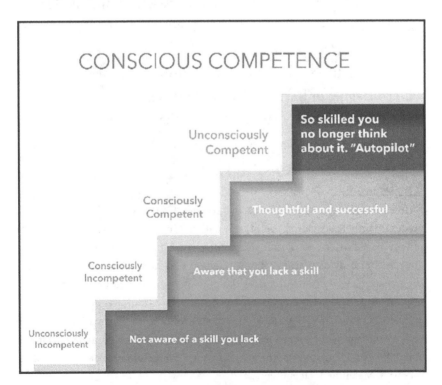

CONSCIOUS COMPETENCE

Unconsciously Competent — So skilled you no longer think about it. "Autopilot"

Consciously Competent — Thoughtful and successful

Consciously Incompetent — Aware that you lack a skill

Unconsciously Incompetent — Not aware of a skill you lack

I emphasize and recommend thoughtful planning for:

- Being crystal clear about your objective
- Using the first 90 seconds to get you and your client aligned
- Creating the best environment for a conversation
- Putting forth the most confident and persuasive version of yourself.

One thing that's worth special mention here, especially in light of the seismic shift our culture is undergoing at the time of this writing, is to add *cultural competence* to your skills and awareness. There are volumes written, mostly of late, that address the interplay of cultural differences in a wide variety of settings. The Internet is bulging with helpful information. Use it. It's your responsibility to know your audience, so if cultural differences seem as if they might be an impediment to your being able to clearly communicate your message and interact in a way that promotes trust and respect, you have a little extra preparation to do. [21]

Research the basics about the culture of your audience. Consult with colleagues or learned friends. Don't stereotype. Pay attention to potential gender dynamics. Ensure that all parties are on the same page about process and expectations. Explain your decision-making process and ask for theirs.

---

[21] Here's an example. When I was a lay preacher, I was asked to fill the pulpit at a predominantly Black church, on Martin Luther King Sunday, no less. The hazards of a privileged white man, a stranger, turning in a cringe worthy performance were obvious. I already clap on 2 & 4, but I had no idea how the spirit moved in this congregation. So, I scouted services the previous Sunday and heard the call and response was the same as every Baptist or AME service I had attended. Nothing too unique. That week, I wrote a long-forgotten sermon titled, 'One nation under the bed.' My fervent wish was just to speak from the heart, with love, and to avoid the temptation to tell anyone anything that was not rooted in my experience. It went very well. Meaning, I felt authentic.

This advice may seem basic, but most people don't prepare like this and it shows. When I taught this material to high-level executives, they unfailingly told me they wished they had learned this much earlier in their careers. Don't wait. Start using these tools right away and reap the benefits.

CHAPTER 12

Nonrational Levers of Influence and the Art of Persuasion

In a fast-moving world, we don't have time to rationally think through every decision. That's why our brain creates shortcuts to help us decide.[22] These occur automatically, almost instinctively. We don't think about them rationally and we aren't aware they're happening—because most of the time the shortcuts work. But because they are not the result of mindful reflection, the leave us vulnerable to "bad actors," people who can try to manipulate us into acting against our interests.

To inoculate yourself against that unfortunate occurrence, try the following techniques. You may discover that they help you master a few persuasive techniques of your own. I confess, I love this stuff—specifically, diving into the secret ways that persuasion happens, or what I refer to as the "dark arts." In Robert B. Cialdini's

---

[22] These shortcuts are also called *heuristics*.

Influence: The Psychology of Persuasion, Cialdini, who did three years of "undercover" research, reveals why people comply with other people's requests. He makes the science accessible and managed to write a page-turner to boot. I highly recommend you read it.[23]

---

[23] My first personal observation with nonrational levers of influence occurred in 1988, when the Watervliet Arsenal celebrated its 175th anniversary. The Arsenal is an Army base and top-secret manufacturing facility. I'd lived most of my life nearby but had never seen inside its massive brick walls. A friend of mine had been commissioned to strike special silver coins to sell at the event, which was invitation-only and included a parade and speeches given from a red, white, and blue bunted platform. My friend recruited me to help her set up the booth and haul the merchandise from her car, which was parked a distance away. As I unloaded the car that early Saturday morning, I walked past the Officers Club, a stately brick colonial-style house.

As my friend and I began arranging the coins for display, our booth got an early-bird visitor: Senator Daniel Patrick Moynihan, a personal hero of mine. He was accompanied by one or two aides and was dressed in his standard tweed suit. I was mentally kicking myself for wearing shorts and a t-shirt when the Senator looked up at me and asked me, "Do you have any beer? I would love a beer." It was 9:15 am. Like most people who paid attention to politics, I knew the Senator had Churchillian drinking habits. I instinctively said, "Not here, Senator, but I know where we can find one!"

By this time, a few soldiers and a few officers had gathered silently at a respectful distance from the Senator and his new best friend (me). I walked out of the booth and introduced myself. "Where are we off to, Patrick?" he said. "Senator, we are going to the Officers Club."

If it's not yet clear, I had no authority to deliver on what I had promised. I was a 25-year-old in shorts, and I could see brows starting to furrow on the uniforms. "Shit," I thought briefly, "could I get arrested for this?" But the next thought was, "Fuck it. In for a dime, in for a dollar." I had no authority, but I did have reflected authority, courtesy of my hungover politician. So, I walked with purpose (just like I tell you to do, Annie) and parted the skeptical GIs as if I were fucking Moses. I don't recall what small talk I made, but I stuck to Moynihan's side and gestured with an air of familiarity, keeping the army guys away from me.

When we reached the Officers Club, I stepped ahead of the Senator to open the door.

Cialdini outlines six basic psychological principles that we tend to use as shortcuts, and which can be exploited for persuading others or letting others persuade us: reciprocity, scarcity, consistency, social proof, likability, and authority.

➤ Reciprocity

It was your grandma who taught me the word *reciprocate*. As a kid, I learned that I could get in about two visits to a friend's house

---

Locked. *Fuuuuck!*

I turned around and an officer finally confronted me, asking in a stern voice, "What are you doing?" In an equally impatient voice, I retorted, "I'm getting the Senator a beer and the door is locked. Can you open it, or do I need to speak with someone else?" The captain's visage was as wrought as a first-timer at the high-stakes poker table. Finally, he folded and opened the door. I led the way to the bar and went to open the cooler.

Padlocked. No sweat this time.

I adopted a bemused look and scanned the uniforms for the least incredulous face. "It's locked," I said. And then I shut up and smiled. (One, one thousand, two, one thousand, three, one…) "I'll take care of it. I've got some beer in my quarters," that person said, breaking the silence. And in a matter of moments, she returned with a six-pack of… Bud Light. All that trouble, I thought, for a goddamn light beer. After having most of a beer with the legendary wit that was DPM, I noticed that the collective amount of brass on the assembled chests was getting weighty. It was time for me to vamoose.

So ended my first lesson in nonrational persuasion. I had unwittingly, but successfully, pulled the authority lever and had a bottle of shit beer with one of America's most celebrated intellectuals.

That was a fun day, but it pales when compared with the two times, in successive years that you (Jack) and I talked our way through two or three layers of security to visit the Cardinals broadcast booth when they were playing the Mets at Citi Field. (There is photographic evidence somewhere.) I smile thinking back to the second year, where you played a key role in getting past the second gatekeeper. Well done, son!

before your grandma insisted that we host the next get-together at ours—with freshly baked cookies, always.

It wasn't that my mom was trying to one-up the other mothers. She was merely adhering to the science that shows that our desire to not be indebted to another is hardwired within us. Let's say that 5,000 years ago, you and your family lived in a cave, next door to another family. If your neighbor killed some game one week, and you had no food, they would share it with you, knowing you'd return the favor. If you didn't return the favor, you might be ostracized—or at least never again be the beneficiary of this family's generosity. And it's from this fear—that we will be banished from the safety of the herd, so to speak—that the psychological need to reciprocate arises.

Cialdini wrote about how back in the 1970s, the Hare Krishnas used the reciprocation principle to great effect when they handed out roses in airports and to passersby on the street. As annoyed as some recipients were, many others made donations to escape the feeling that they now owed these people something.

Jack: You may recall coming to my office in New York City a few years ago. I suggested we go outside and see if we could replicate Cialdini's Hare Krishna experiment. What made this interesting was that we experienced an updated strategy, which included other nonrational persuasive levers. In case you don't remember the encounter, a smiling monk, looking splendid in maroon and saffron robes, would typically stake out the corner of 5th Avenue and 42nd Street, in front of the New York Public Library. When he caught my eye that afternoon (easy to do since you and I intended to participate) he approached, holding out a shiny, multicolored badge. When I reached out to accept, he slipped a handsome bracelet of wooden beads on my wrist. Two gifts!

What came next was not the ask for a donation. Instead, the

monk asked me what I would like the monks to pray for. As he asked, he opened a black leather-bound notebook and handed it to me. The page had three columns. He asked me to put down my first name and my prayer in the first two columns. When I tried to hand the book back, he shook his head and pointed insistently at the third column, where I was to write down the amount of my contribution.

I had been prepared to give him five bucks for the lesson in persuasion, but I was astounded to see that all of the others on the page had purportedly given either $20 or $50. Without requesting a specific amount, he essentially opened the bidding with a high anchor by showing me the (invented) high amounts given by others. He also used the principle of social proof: showing me that people like me had given at a high level. The unspoken message was clear: Cough up $50 just like Frank and Mark and everyone else on the list. I think we gave him $10, a fair price for the psychology class.

What should you do with this information? First, understand that when you occasionally go on autopilot, certain people or groups may try to work the principle of reciprocity against you. That's why it's important to cultivate a habit of asking yourself if the gift you are receiving is being given freely, or if there are ulterior motives. This entails taking a brief moment to step back and consider what's happening (akin to watching the thinker, as I described earlier). As you do this, think about whether you actually want to give back anything at all, or if you feel compelled because the other person is a good manipulator.

On the other hand, it's also possible to use reciprocity to your advantage, though it's a Machiavellian thing to do. It can also put a big dent in your credibility if you're too obvious about it; people do not like being manipulated. In my view, it's far easier to cultivate the habit espoused by my late friend, Red Hat Bill. His motto was

"Ask for help; help when asked." I've found that if you help others and grant favors easily, it all works out fine in the end.

And it's even better if you don't wait to be asked. Doing nice things unbidden is a great credibility builder. Plus, it feels good. To my mind, it's always best to use your awareness of the reciprocity principle as a shield against the unscrupulous, rather than a tool that advances a scheme.[24]

➤ Scarcity

The scarcity principle is more intuitive. When something is hard to obtain, we desire it more, typically because we have a fear of missing out (FOMO).

The desire for something scarce is compounded if the buyer believes only a few people know about it. In one experiment, when shoppers were told of a limited-time sale on meat, they bought three times more than did a group who was told there was no time limit. And when told that only a select few knew about the sale, shoppers bought six times more meat than those unaware of either limit.

Simple as it seems, two conditions need to be present for the scarcity principle to work:

First, we tend to want something more if its availability has recently decreased than if it has remained steady over time. Second, competition, or the fear of losing something to a rival, makes us more zealous to secure the opportunity, or to buy what's on offer.

My favorite example involves a young man who would buy used

---

[24] A nice example of how this occurs naturally is well known to you, Anne. Recall I did a favor for a friend and set up a meeting for his nephew. They found it helpful, and two years later, when I asked for a favor in return—a meeting of much higher "value"—it was granted without question. The moral of the story is to do as much good for as many people as you can.

cars, detail and fix them up, and resell them. His trick was to double- or triple-up appointments to see the car. If the appointed time was Sunday at 2 PM, he would have two or three prospective buyers looking at the car at the same time, thus ensuring a competitive environment and fueling a competition where no one wanted to be left out.

To counter the eagerness that arises from scarcity, we should, again, take a minute to mentally step back and ask if we truly want the item, or if we are being manipulated by its perceived scarcity. Which brings us back to conscious competence—the most reliable vantage point when making decisions.

➤ Commitment and Consistency

If we make a commitment, particularly a public one, we are more apt to try to be consistent with that pledge.

Most of us also like being seen as a person of our word, as someone others view as reliable and able to stick with a decision once we've made it.

Unlike the reciprocity principle, which I find too manipulative to use to persuade someone, commitment and consistency are appropriate tools and ones I have employed often—say, whenever I remind others of a position they've previously taken.

The conversation might go like this:

ME: Mr. Donor, when we met last month, you expressed disappointment with the carbon footprint for our new patient service center and stated that going forward, you would make philanthropic gifts only for projects that were environmentally responsible. Did I understand that correctly?

DONOR: Yes, that's correct.

ME: Excellent. We met with an energy specialist and made a number of changes to our plans. I'm happy to report that we are on track to be awarded platinum LEED certification, which, as you know, is the highest designation for commercial buildings. Today, we would like to thank you for pointing us in that direction, and to begin a conversation with you about a personal gift to our project.

I'm reluctant to even call this manipulation, since I consider it fair play to take someone at their word. I've also found this tool to be effective in showing that I was listening well to what was said and took it to heart.

Besides, the person can always change their mind, which is what I encourage you to do if someone tries to use your prior position to persuade you of something.

For example, the donor might have said, "I am committed to environmentally responsible building, but that is just one of several issues I have with what you have planned."

➢ Social Proof

This principle simply reminds us that we often make decisions based on what other people are doing.

My best personal example came at the end of my third year of law school, when, after procrastinating, I had to hurry up and pick a bar review course that very afternoon. As I looked at the three vendors set up in the cafeteria, I saw that vendors A and B had lines of between two and five students waiting to sign up, which meant

I could sign up without a wait. The line for the third vendor, Bar-Bri, stretched out of the cafeteria and down a hallway. It would be at least an hour's wait.

Guess which course I chose?

Given that I saw a lot of very smart students in the Bar-Bri line, I figured that if it was good enough for those folks, it was good enough for me. Back then, I would have called it safety in numbers. Due to my procrastination, I had not investigated any of the courses, so I was very uncertain about which to choose. And according to Cialdini, social proof works best when the decider is uncertain due to a lack of information.

As you've probably realized by now, we use social proof all the time. Laugh tracks on sitcoms cue us to laugh; the piano player at the bar stuffs a few bills in the cognac snifter before he starts playing; the monk represents that the smallest donation is $20; marketers throw around phrases like "best-selling" or "fastest-growing" to make customers feel that others are buying the products too. And social proof explains why teenagers, while professing their uniqueness, tend to follow the herd in what they wear and do.

Here is my second favorite example of marketers applying psychological principles to their work:

Readers of a certain age will remember the advent of television infomercials with the tagline "Operators are standing by, please call now." I never paid any conscious attention to those words, but the brilliant marketer Colleen Szot did. She asked, "What mental images are conjured up by the words *operators are waiting*?

The answer? A call center filled with operators who were waiting—maybe filing their nails or playing solitaire while they cooled their heels by their silent telephones. In other words, the image suggests that nobody is calling—not very helpful when you are trying to persuade people to make an impulse purchase.

Szot changed the game by switching out "Operators are waiting, please call now" to "If operators are busy, please call again," which resulted in a 20-year sales record being broken. Now viewers imagined operators being inundated with calls, which was apparently enough to convince people on the fence about buying that others like them were calling too.

➤ Likability

We enjoy working with, and are more apt to follow the lead of, people we like.

Good salespeople do a good job of being likable. They understand that all of us appreciate sincere compliments or thanks for a job well done or a positive reaction to something we've said, along the lines of "That's a great idea!" or "Interesting point."

We are also affected by the degree to which we have things in common with another person—and the more unusual or detailed the things, the better. I still remember when my friend Amy Montaldo discovered that we both loved and frequently reread an obscure book, *Illusions*, by Richard Bach. An important caveat, however, is that we have to be sure our preference for people who are similar to us doesn't inadvertently perpetuate patriarchy and privilege. Be deliberate in growing the diversity of your world.

We also like it when people make the effort to keep a friendship going. (One regret I have is that I didn't maintain contact with as many good people as I might have.) And never, ever underestimate the power of a handwritten note.

Finally, take a lesson from what you've doubtless experienced yourselves. Imagine that you're at a party and the person on your left is talking incessantly about himself, while the person on the right is asking questions about you. Who would you be more drawn to? Hint: We all like talking about ourselves.

All of this adds up to the likability effect, which is compounded if we find the person physically attractive. People tend to see attractive people as smart, kind, and honest. Sadly, this extends to politics as well; all things being equal, the good-looking candidate tends to prevail.

Yet another especially powerful factor in our liking someone is when we're cooperating for some shared goal or see the person as being on the same team. Good cop/bad cop interrogation only works if the suspect perceives the good cop is standing up for him and is an ally he can trust.

The interesting thing is, if you find you've developed a strong liking for a person or thing in a short period of time, that's not necessarily a good thing. On the contrary, red flags should go up. Ask yourself the reasons for this sudden infatuation.

➢ Authority

We tend to obey authority figures without question (think: doctors or police), and these symbols of authority may have such a strong hypnotic effect on us that we don't bother to think or challenge before obeying.

Renowned psychologist Stanley Milgram conducted a study in the 1960s showing that volunteers would administer what they thought were potentially lethal electric shocks to others simply because they were told to do so by an authority figure. Although no one was harmed, the experimenters were startled by how easy it was to get these graduate students to act sadistically.

Clothes and props that look like symbols of authority can bolster our irrational response. In Milgram's experiment, it was the authority figure's white lab coat and clipboard that convinced participants they should obey them and "torture" their fellow test subjects.

So how can we inoculate ourselves against this kind of manipulation?

Being aware of the power of authority is a good first step. Also, there are two questions you should ask before jumping to obey:

First, is this person really an authority or merely masquerading as one? Are their credentials valid for the situation at hand? Or have they simply donned a white lab coat to appear to be a doctor, as actor Robert Young did when he was shilling for Sanka coffee? (He played Dr. Marcus Welby on television—I know, before your time!) Here, simply asking if his credentials were valid for recommending a brand of coffee would have revealed him as a false authority.

The second question is to ask yourself whether the person has your best interests at heart. A waiter, for example, may be an expert on the wine list at a restaurant, but he also stands to gain from recommending more expensive wines.

➤ The Power of Because

Ellen Langer, who is still doing the coolest brain science research at Harvard, made her name with a 1978 study that has been dubbed The Copy Machine Experiment. (The actual title of her paper was killer: "Mindlessness of Ostensibly Thoughtful Action.")

You can read the study yourselves if you are a nerd like me. The citation is in the appendix. But the upshot is that if you provide a reason for a request ("Can I use the copy machine before you because I'm in a rush?"), you stand a far greater chance of having your request granted, even if the reason is a poor one.

In the study, researchers would attempt to cut the line to use the lone copy machine in a university library, using requests worded three different ways.

"May I skip the line?" (no reason given)—60% of people agreed to the request.

"May I skip the line because I'm in a rush?"—94 percent of people complied.

But, fascinatingly, if a nonsensical reason was given—"May I skip the line because I need to make copies?"—93 percent still complied. I loved teaching this lesson. My clients' mouths would drop open every time. "WTF?!" was a customary response.

Bottom line: When making a request, give a reason.

> CHAPTER 13

Conversational Excellence

T he best meetings are driven by excellent conversation. At my
last consultancy, Templar Advisors, our core thesis was that
natural, relaxed conversation is a model of excellence, albeit one
that is uniquely personal (everyone has their own conversational
style). One thing I did as a consultant was to help clients access
their authentic, conversational voices to best communicate with
and persuade others. Ideally, that means a two-way dialogue with
lots of Q&A, where key points are practical and focused on the
client's interests.[25]

Maybe this seems like a blinding flash of the obvious. But
I feel strongly about sharing some universal tips and tricks for

---

[25] I was continually surprised by how many clients told me that simply having a
meeting like the one described above was enough to make them stand out from the
competition—that Holy Grail known as *differentiation*. The number one complaint
in business is too many bad meetings, but with a little discipline and preparation
you guys can learn to run efficient and productive meetings with confidence and
ease.

conducting a good conversation that cut across personality types. Following these tips will help you not only be more persuasive (and successful) but also remain authentically comfortable and able to express yourself in pressure situations.

If you look at the art of conversation from 10,000 feet, what's clear is that there are three main objectives in every conversation: to inform, to get whoever you are talking with to engage with you, and to persuade them to do something (if that happens to be your aim).

1. **Inform.** This refers to the stuff you're there to talk about. Limit yourself to two or three key points, because they won't retain more. One of the biggest mistakes people make, at least in meetings, is to try to impart too much information. This was my problem early in my career. One of my strengths is the ability to see things whole, to see how parts are interconnected. I would speak at length to demonstrate the elegance of the system in my head. One boss told me that by explaining everything in my head, it seemed as if I was trying to show how smart I was. Yikes! That was feedback I needed to hear only once. To ensure that you get your two or three points across, you must express them in terms of the benefit to the other person, using *So what?* or *WIIFM?* language, as I explained earlier.

2. **Engage.** Engagement happens during your interaction with the other person; merely imparting information isn't enough. When conversations/pitches are unsuccessful, it's almost always because the engagement element is lacking. I talk about this in detail below.

3. **Move.** The third conversational objective is to make movement happen—to get to an agreement of some kind. That agreement could be as simple as a teacher letting a

student turn in a paper a day late, or as significant as a firm persuading a client to approve a big deal. My former boss and colleague, Karen Osborne, called this "getting to the joyful yes,"[26] and it also involves explicitly laying out the benefits, truly connecting, building the relationship, developing trust, and feeling confidence in your own message.

The best measure of a successful meeting is how engaging the client finds you. Here are a few tips for accomplishing that:

- **Consider your pace,** which is the rate of your words and, more important, the rate of your idea presentation. Actually, don't worry too much about your rate of words, since listeners can process around 180 words per minute and not even an excited Italian talks that fast.[27] Plus, a brisk rate of words is seen (and heard) as energy and enthusiasm.

- **Keep in mind the power of the pause,** even when you're under pressure. The most damaging problem is the rate at which people present their ideas. When someone "talks too fast," it's not that they are speaking too many words; it's that there are too few conversational pauses in between those words. You don't need to pause for a long time, maybe 1.5 to 3 seconds, but a lot of good, important stuff happens in those little gaps. The trouble is, when we feel under pressure, maybe because we dislike public speaking or are unprepared, we tend to rush our delivery and shorten or

---

[26] Over our brief time working together, Karen sent me three handwritten notes, and I remember each one, lest you're not convinced that such notes make an impression.
[27] Although, Anne, when you were hanging with your friends in high school, I think you might have set the American record for rate of words! My God, you girls were incomprehensible, except to each other. Perhaps that was the idea.

eliminate those pauses.[28] That's understandable. Once a little adrenaline hits the system, our perception of time passing slows down, making a normal conversational pause feel like an eternity—an eternity we fill with verbal tics (*ums, ers, kind ofs*) to get ourselves the hell out of that uncomfortable moment of silence. It's a bad habit, and one you have to break to be a good communicator. But if you resist the urge to fill those pauses, you'll discover how vitally important they really are. For one thing, the brain cannot listen and comprehend at exactly the same time. We need a little bit of time to process, which is where those pauses come in. Take them away and the listener has to work harder to keep up and comprehend. One thing I discovered is that if I could get a client who was having a hard time making himself understood because of a heavy accent to slow down his rate of idea presentation and insert more pauses, he was easily understood. We all need time to process. The pause, coupled with eye contact, actually asks your audience a question: *Did you get that?* Most often, the client will nod (or, if on the phone, grunt), indicating that they're following and that it's okay to move ahead. Or perhaps they'll use the pause to ask a question. All of these things clue us in to the fact that they are engaged. And if you get a blank stare or hear no grunt on the phone, it might be good to directly ask the person if they're with you—something along the lines of, *Make sense? So far so*

---

[28] I've long heard the axiom that most people fear public speaking more than death, so I went in search of a proper study to substantiate that bizarre conclusion. A Google search revealed nothing, but the percentages are consistently high—around 45%. But the main reason for this footnote is to retell a Jerry Seinfeld dad joke. He said that if you fear public speaking more than death, and you have to go to a funeral, you'd be better off in the casket than delivering the eulogy.

good? Use these sparingly, however, lest you appear to be talking down to your audience.

- **Don't forget about eye contact.** The biggest upside of pausing is the chance to make eye contact. Punctuating key points with a combination of eye contact and silence projects confidence, truthfulness, and authority. If you're comfortable pausing and making eye contact, you'll have mastered the most important components of successful communication. It helps to remember that even if silence makes you uneasy, on a subconscious level, at least, your audience will feel relief that they have a moment to process, or to ask you a question and get further engaged. Not that looking someone in the eye is easy, especially if the person is older and more experienced than you are. More often than not, though, we fail to make eye contact because we are looking down at our notes to tee up our next point. But whatever the reason, clients interpret lack of eye contact the same way: that the person talking lacks conviction and may be a bit shifty. The amount of eye contact depends on whether you are speaking or listening. Listeners should be giving 100% eye contact. If you are speaking, on the other hand, it's more a question of timing. Pausing with eye contact after delivering a point emphasizes what you are saying while giving you a chance to gauge the client's reaction. When you are speaking, you should never give any one person an excessive amount of eye contact. Share the love, look around; they only need eye contact on those key points. (We've all been in one-on-one meetings where it feels like the person speaking is trying to bore a hole in our head.)

- **As far as body language goes, less is more.** There is a lot of shit science out there on the subject (if you look up to the left, you had eggs for breakfast).[29] I like to keep it simple. Whether sitting or standing, mind your posture and don't fidget (e.g., flip your pen or fuss with your hair). You don't need to become a mannequin; by all means, move around naturally. If you are seated, start off leaning forward a bit, put your hands on the table in front of you, and put them into play. Be yourself. And if you are standing, forget the leaning forward part, or you might lose your balance! You may also want to avoid crossing your arms, since it projects a message of defensiveness, though what it really means is anyone's guess. (I tell clients not to read too much into it if an audience member crosses their arms.)

- **Let mirroring happen naturally.** Sometimes, people who have been through cheesy sales programs will ask if they should actively mirror the client's gestures and expressions. (I once had a subject show me what he meant by mirroring, and it felt like a bad mime show.) There is some research that suggests we feel more comfortable with those who roughly match us in tone and posture. But my take is that mirroring happens naturally because humans are natural mimics. If you focus on it too much, you'll get distracted from what's most important: having a conversation in the moment.

- **Keep your language simple.** I once heard a senior executive say, "In order to facilitate the trans-departmental syndication of information." I'm pretty sure he meant that he wanted others to know what was going on. While you

---

[29] Hat tip to my dear friend and colleague, Hugo Williams. Hugo relentlessly pushed me to speak plainly. I once used the phrase "surreptitious videotaping" and he shuddered. "We call that sneaky filming," he replied. A Brit right out of central casting, he once responded to a suggestion that we dine at 6:00 PM with, "Do I look like a fucking mailman from Des Moines? I'll see you at half seven for drinks."

may be tempted to use big words, most of the time you'll end up sounding silly. Go with plain, everyday language. Avoid the temptation to "formalize" your language and sentence structure when speaking or presenting to clients.

- **Minimize acronyms** unless you are sure the audience will understand them. And above all, never use jargon. In fact, if anyone calls you out for sounding like an empty suit, buy them lunch. They've done you a big favor.

One day, during the Manhattan Hope Lodge period, I was on a weekly conference call with my deal team, which comprised about ten NYC lawyers and real estate guys. By that time, abuse of the meaningless phrase "at the end of the day" had reached an epic level. I couldn't take much more. I tallied up the number of times the phrase was used during the call. At the end, I recapped action items and then asked the group if I'd missed anything, confessing that I had been distracted by the 27 times (!) the offending phrase had been used.

I've compiled a list of some annoying jargon words, and some better alternatives:

Eye-roll inducing	Understandable
Let's touch base	Can we meet?
Paradigm shift	We see it differently
Disrupt	Improve
Leverage	Use
Synergize	Work together
In the pipeline	Haven't done it yet
Buy-in	Support

The good news is that communication styles are eminently fixable. My tips will help a little. What will help a lot is practicing your public- and group-speaking skills. Happily, you won't have to spend 10,000 hours on them to become expert, as Malcolm Gladwell might suggest. At Templar, we made extensive use of video recording. It can be uncomfortable as hell to see and hear yourself as you actually appear to others. But I have seen people improve dramatically after just a few tapings, in less than a day.

So use your smartphone camera for something other than Instagram. Think of a familiar subject, prop your camera up, hit video, and pretend you're explaining that familiar subject to a friend. When you review the video, check for rate of ideas, pauses, eye contact, posture, fidgeting, and, if you're pitching something, your use of benefit language. Finally, if you have a serious fear of public speaking, try Toastmasters. I frequently recommend it to clients who want more practice in front of a live audience. It's dirt cheap and I've never heard a bad review.

> CHAPTER 14

Smart Starts

E arly in my career, the transition from small talk to the business
part of the meeting often felt uncomfortable, especially when
addressing someone older than I was—which was almost always
the case.[30]

The discomfort got into my head and I felt self-conscious and
nervous, which affected my confidence. I struggled to converse
naturally and failed to project authority and gravitas. I noticed
that when I did get off to a good start, I had better meetings. I soon

---

[30] Micro-lesson: My first job, working for newspaper publishers, took me to some
fancy meeting locations with a bunch of old, rich white men. Before my first board
meeting, I agonized about how to gain the respect of these guys. I was 20 years old,
trying to present as something other than a coffee boy. The most intimidating man
was Roy Park, who owned a chain of newspapers. Indelibly etched in my memory
is me standing up in the *New York Times* executive dining room upon his arrival,
extending my hand in introduction, and saying, "I'm Patrick McKenna, pleased to
meet you, Roy." To which he replied, with a nearly imperceptible raised eyebrow,
"Pleased to meet you…Mr. McKenna." That's the kind of shit that wound me around
the axle, early on. Don't be like me. Until you for certain know differently, always
address people who are a generation older than you as "Mr." or "Ms." until they
invite you to call them by their first names.

realized that good starts were preceded by planning. So, I made an adjustment.

I discovered that if I spent 10 to 20 minutes beforehand clarifying my key points and objectives, I felt less anxious. I began looking forward to meetings rather than feeling butterflies. Some years later, I refined my planning to explicitly include the benefits clients would get out of the meeting.

Planning the first two minutes of a conversation or presentation will lead to better meetings. If you plan or rehearse nothing else, at least do this. The dividends of nailing the first two minutes are huge and easily attained.

There are thousands of websites or consultants with advice on starting meetings, but the best tool I've encountered (and used to great effect) was developed by my colleagues at Templar Advisors. They call it PPPC (for Purpose, Process, Pay-off, and Check). I found it inspired and useful in nearly every context. It's the Swiss Army knife of tools for smart starts. A well-executed PPPC subtly puts you in charge and answers several unasked questions for your client, makes them feel good about the meeting (or your piece of it), and gets you into a two-way dialogue quickly and naturally.

Be aware of the following:

- Don't go on too long. Ideally, these introductory bits should last no longer than 90 seconds, and I've seen good ones take as little as 30 seconds.
- These structures work very well even when you are not leading the meeting but have just a short piece.
- This is NOT your presentation. Be specific but stay out of the weeds.

- Regardless of the structure you use to frame your opening, do not give short shrift to small talk beforehand.[31] Clients generally expect a little chitchat, unless you're in New York City, where small talk is often not much more than "Whaddaya got?"[32] Otherwise, small talk is a great way to build rapport. Remember, likability is important in gaining trust (and a client's business).

To illustrate how smart starts work, imagine this scenario:

You are a busy bank president who guards his calendar carefully, but because a close associate asked, you have agreed to a meeting with an executive of a local charity. Your associate mentioned that they were thinking of you as a possible chairperson for a capital campaign. You aren't terribly keen, given your last such engagement was a chaotic slog that took longer than expected and barely made its goal. Regardless, you said you would keep an open mind and penciled thirty minutes into your diary.

---

[31] I recall a meeting my colleague, Diana Martin, had with a key new constituent. We waited in the lobby for 30 minutes after our appointed time, and when we got in his office, all signs pointed to this guy wanting to get down to business. I had just opened my mouth to kick off the substantive part of the meeting when I felt Diana's hand clamp down on my right knee, like she was giving me a horse bite on the playground. "Oh, my! Are those your grandchildren, John?" John's countenance changed immediately, and for the next ten minutes he gave us a guided tour of his progeny, along with helpful insights into his values and priorities. Thanks to Diana, that relationship bloomed, and I relearned a valuable lesson about the importance of at least trying to build a little rapport at the top of each meeting.

[32] Culture has a lot to do with the quality and importance of small talk. My Latin American clients regaled me with tales of the social part of the meeting lasting for hours, sometimes late into the night, before it was time to discuss business.

➢ All-Purpose Smart Start Structure (PPPC)

Purpose: "Mr. Jones, it's good to be with you. My colleague, Jack McKenna, and I are excited[33] for this opportunity to share with you the results of the analysis about the feasibility of our capital campaign and to reiterate our strong desire that you serve as its chair."

Here you simply remind your client of what the meeting is about. Don't take for granted that they know or remember; they are busy people!

Notice the absence of "thank you for your time" or any of its variations. Throwaway phrases like those are meaningless. Everyone uses them, and no one really means them. Plus, phrases like these subtly send a message that the other person's time is more valuable than yours. Even if there is a vast power difference, you don't help yourself by emphasizing that. There are countless other better phrases that place you on a more peer-to-peer footing, such as "good to be with you," "glad we could find the time," etc. If you feel compelled to thank them for their time, wait until you're saying goodbye.

Process: "We've brought the consultant's report, but we're not going to drag you through it. We'll leave a copy with you for later reference. What I propose is that I spend five to seven minutes covering the key findings, and then I'll turn it over to Jack, who's been having some initial conversations with prospective lead donors that you'll find interesting. Please jump in with questions at any time, and I know you have a call at 3 PM, so let's call a hard stop at 2:45."

---

[33] If you are nervous going into a meeting, you should know that reframing your anxiety as excitement will make you perform better. Anxiety and excitement share many of the same physiological traits (elevated heart rate, butterflies, etc.), but excitement is positive, whereas anxiety is not. A Harvard study that established this great trick is cited in the appendix.

Clients love this part because it puts them at ease. They need to understand what will happen. And they need to know what is expected of them. An explanation of the process subtly tells them how to behave. And if everyone is on the same page, they will feel more comfortable and more focused, and will contribute more effectively. Finally, nobody wants to get dragged through a report they could read on their own, so letting them know you won't do that makes you even more likable!

Payoff: Mr. Jones, by the end of the meeting, we believe you'll take away three key points. First, that there is a clear and well-documented basis for why a campaign is needed; second, that with your leadership, we can raise $100 million in as little as 12 months; and lastly, if you do choose to serve as chair, we can assemble a team to support you at every turn, thus ensuring a good use of your time."

The payoff tells them the benefit of having the meeting. It's a bit like WIIFM, but instead of focusing on the benefit of being the campaign chair, it assures the client that this meeting will be time well spent.

Most people don't include a payoff in their introduction, and that's a big missed opportunity. Giving them the payoff up front tells the client what to listen for, meaning your top messages have a better chance of getting through.

Finally, by putting the benefits up front, the client will not be surprised when you make the formal ask at the end.

Check: "How does that sound for an agenda?" (or words to that effect)

This part is easy to forget, but don't. Keep the check brief and be quiet after you ask. You will get one of two responses. Either the client will say it sounds fine (which will make you happy, because early agreement in a meeting is a confidence boost), or they may want to change something, which is also great because it's explicitly revealing an area of interest to them. Just make an agreed-upon adjustment to your process and proceed.

Finally, the check creates an implicit agreement that makes it less likely that your agenda will get hijacked by another topic, or that you'll have to deal with pushback later on.

➢ A Structure to Tee Up Dialogue (SCQ-S)

Another smart start structure is a variant of a McKinsey presentation model developed by their first female partner, Barbara Minto. McKinsey calls this Situation – Complication – Resolution, and it continues to be used today when McKinsey presents its final recommendations during an engagement.

Templar Advisors adroitly modified this framework to serve as an introductory structure that can be used in situations where you want dialogue with the client to become the centerpiece of the meeting. Templar's version is Situation – Complication – Questions (with your proposed Solution in your back pocket, in the hope that the solution emerges naturally in conversation with the client as a result of the questions posed).

To illustrate SCQ-S, imagine you are the banker (now campaign chair) and I've come to your office for a meeting ten months later.

Situation: "I'm glad we could do this update in person. We are thrilled that we hit the $90 million mark this month. I would also be remiss if I didn't thank you for the introduction to Mr. Bardin. His was an unexpected gift, and it came at an opportune time. Look, you've seen all the reports and know we are ahead of all our benchmarks."

In other words, the "Situation" is a fact-based statement about the current state of affairs about which no one could disagree. It's purely objective and provides the context for what comes next. Try to make it a rosy, upbeat message, highlighting the positives. If possible, without blowing smoke up your client's ass, compliment them for their accomplishments. You want this part to be positive because coming next is the…

Complication: "But, as you know, we were counting on Lashawnda Morgan for the gift that would take us over the line and complete the campaign. Due to her recent indictment, I think she'll be devoting those funds to legal fees. Thus, we have to come up with a plan to fill this gap. Because if we don't reach $100 million by September, our construction costs may increase."

The Complication is what you are there to solve—it's the focus of the meeting and the issue you are addressing (e.g., "We need a new plan to finish the campaign."). It lays out why some action is needed, why something needs to change. Don't be shy here. Be explicit about the pain that will be incurred if a solution isn't found.

Again, you want your explication to be as objective and incontrovertible as possible, so you don't get interrupted. Because what comes next is where your value starts to appear in the form of thoughtful, well-constructed…

Questions: "So the questions we'd like to discuss with you today are about how we can close the gap and bring the campaign to a successful end. First, what might be the reaction of our lead donors if we went back to them and asked them to help us close the gap; second, what would it take to move the public phase of the campaign forward by two months; and lastly, what shall our communication strategy be for all our donors once this challenge becomes public?"

By using this structure, you are setting discussion of these questions as the agenda. At this point, I do a quick check with the client (e.g. "How does that sound?). Assuming a positive response, dive right into the first question.

Your content is communicated through your side of the conversation. Clients will sometimes turn the tables and ask for your thoughts first, so be prepared. Above all, craft your questions carefully and in advance. This is no time to wing it. You want to ask smart questions that point generally to solutions that you are capable of implementing.

Solution: Unless the client asks for a solution up front (and some will), I prefer to let the solution emerge from the conversation elicited by the questions. This way, the client feels that they contributed and will be more committed to the resulting decision than they would be if the solution was just dropped in their lap. In the capital campaign example, I cared less about the details of the solution; I was far more interested in the chairperson being fully committed to its implementation.

> CHAPTER 15

Public Speaking: Nothing to Fear Here

A bit more preparation is usually required when it comes to public speaking. When speaking publicly, you want to ensure that you say all you want to say, and no more. To do that, you need a proper set of notes, by which I mean somewhere between a script and nothing. Remember my crappy acceptance speech in law school? I had no notes. Today I can ad-lib with the best of them, but that has taken years of practice and enough comfort with silence that I'm able to take a minute to gather my thoughts. Early in my career, I recall a couple of occasions where I started speaking in a meeting but ended up meandering about, my point lost because I had no through line. I ended up saying things I hadn't intended to say. I couldn't get out of the rabbit holes I dug for myself. The laughter from the critical committee in my head was deafening.

That's when I learned that speaking without notes is high-risk. Some people who appear to be speaking extemporaneously have memorized their script, which is even more dangerous. I've seen businesspeople and actors "go up" on their lines and hemorrhage credibility.[34]

At the other extreme is relying on a script. I've had no fewer than three bosses who presented at board meetings by reading a written report prepared in advance: head down, word for word. And worse, their remarks were distributed days earlier, so for many board members, the recitations were not just agonizing, but useless. They were universally awful performances, but since the presenters were all glued to their prepared remarks, they couldn't see the reaction they were getting. I, however, could see the members' faces and body language. It was not encouraging. These presentations were all monologues. The presenters missed all the cues, including some affirming head nods and smiles from more positive members. Nor were there any natural pauses that might have allowed for questions.

Nobody likes being read to; it's only a marginal improvement on watching a beginners' improv class. Except when giving a formal speech from a lectern to a group of more than 40, stay away from scripts, and even then, be sure your script is professionally edited.

---

[34] I'm sometimes asked if my training as an actor helped make me a better public speaker. It certainly helped me get used to being in front of large groups, but it didn't add much to my coaching. Nor did I mention my acting experience when marketing my services. Non-actors tend to view acting as playing make-believe or being inauthentic. Nothing could be further from the truth, of course. But changing minds on that point confuses the objective of a marketing or sales meeting. The candle isn't worth the game. My approach to acting is best captured by James Cagney: "Hit your mark, look the other fellow in the eye, and tell the truth." Tell the truth as it is for your character would be more accurate. Funny story: In the movie *Marathon Man*, Dustin Hoffman's character is about to be tortured by a Nazi war criminal turned dentist, played by Laurence Olivier. A consummate Method actor, Hoffman prepared for the scene by depriving himself of sleep for days to fully embody his character. When he turned up to film the scene, he looked like shit. When he told Olivier how he prepared, Sir Laurence famously suggested that it would be easier for Hoffman if he tried acting.

Another common mistake: When preparing for a presentation, too many people start by constructing PowerPoint slides or pitch books. This is a huge waste of time. If you want to present authentically and effectively, *think about your slides last.* Better yet, forget about them. Ask yourself if you really need them. Because the truth is, if your presentation hinges on your slides or other printed materials, you have a problem; as soon as you stop engaging with your audience and watch them read instead, you've lost control of the meeting.

Instead of starting your preparation with PowerPoint, just scribble down a skeleton of what you want to say in your presentation—main argument; key points; and relevant data, examples, and authorities. From these cocktail-napkin notes you can then build a Word document, putting together your research and collecting thoughts, data, and images, then playing with the structure and flow until you've got a coherent presentation.

Once you're happy with the content, distill it down to a central idea and draw out the three points you want your audience to remember. That's the moment—and no sooner—that you should think about what slides you need to support your presentation, if any. The aim is to eliminate everything superfluous. The emptier, and fewer, your slides, the better. That means no gimmicks, no stock photography.

Instead of PowerPoint, go for notes—a happy medium. In addition to the advice above, the following guidelines have served me well:

- Draft notes in 18-point bold font for easy reading.
- Make your notes simple and logical: a checklist of all the points you wish to make.
- Allow liberal white space and indentations, so you can easily find your place.

- Do not write your notes in complete sentences. Use as few words as possible, just enough to prompt you to remember the point or content you'll speak to next.
- Have enough notes so you don't have to rely on your memory to connect your points.
- Resist the strong temptation to continue speaking when looking down at your notes. Instead, do it this way: Look down silently to get your note. Look up and say what you want to say as concisely, crisply, simply, and briefly as you can. Pause after each point for emphasis and hold eye contact with your audience through the pause. After the pause, look down silently again to get your next note.

Stick to your notes. If you get a brilliant new thought halfway through, jot a note and give it proper consideration when you're finished.

Finally, don't forget to do a full rehearsal. Any important presentation deserves one.

> CHAPTER 16

Eliciting, Answering, and Asking Questions

"It is not the answer that enlightens, but the question."
—*Eugene Ionesco*

"Judge a man by his questions rather than his answers."
—*Voltaire*

The best presentations and pitches evolve into a dialogue, and that happens by eliciting questions.

Questions tell you that your client is listening. Perhaps they just need clarification, but just as often, their questions will point you to something that interests them, or a potential area of concern. It's perfectly fine to probe further ("Is that an area of interest or concern to you? If so, would you help me understand why?"). Just be sure you say this AFTER you respond to the question.

In fact, there are ways to encourage questions.

The best and most important way is to be sure to pause after key points and punctuate those pauses with eye contact. Not only does this emphasize your point, but the "did you get that?" eye contact/ pause gives your client time to interject.

Also, while you must make a strong, persuasive presentation that stands on its own, leave some details out, so your client has an opportunity to raise questions and feel they are contributing.

You can simply ask if anyone has questions, but in my experience, that often results in uncomfortable silence. You could direct a question to an individual, but if they don't know the answer, this can be risky. Instead, I've found that if I'm stuck with a very nonresponsive group, especially when it includes junior people with their boss present, I will ask an attributive question. "Mr. Boss, you've been leading campaigns for more than 20 years. No one knows better than you that the final 10 percent of the goal is the hardest to achieve. So, what are your thoughts on how similar this situation is to what you did at Penn?" This question flatters the target by acknowledging their experience and attributing a degree of expertise to them. However, I use this device only when I'm confident of a helpful answer.

➤ The Wrong Way to Answer Questions

Of course, if you elicit questions, you have to know how to answer them well. I've seen good presentations fall apart because the speaker handled questions poorly. A good benchmark: The quality of your answers should match the quality of your presentation. Attracting questions and answering them well are as important as the presentation itself.

If you're a young professional, you may be especially prone to fumbling questions posed by the audience, if only because you...

- Typically have had fewer opportunities to contribute to, or lead, meetings.

- May be especially eager to impress and let your answers run long. Keep your answers to 45–60 seconds, the shorter the better, without being dismissive or curt.

- Fail to answer directly, instead trying to explain your thinking or, worse, talking while you think as you get to the answer (if you ever do). Go this route and you risk losing the audience's attention. If an answer needs explaining, follow the "bottom line up front" (BLUF) rule. Answer the question directly (yes, no, maybe so) and then provide any supporting data, keeping your answer under a minute. If the questioner needs more information, they will ask. If they get impatient with the back and forth, you can offer to explain with all the details. Just forewarn them that they'll be getting the "long version," or offer to speak with them later.

- Begin answering immediately. This can make you appear dismissive or, God forbid, as if you're interrupting the questioner, which is simply rude. Be sure to pause, give due consideration to the query and your response, then answer the question.

- Have failed to prepare answers to foreseeable questions, especially the difficult ones. As noted earlier, a few minutes of consciously competent preparation can make a difference. Workshop your answers with a colleague to ensure a tight, powerful response.

- Bluff your way through an answer. I've seen people try to bluff, and they've gone up in flames. Nobody expects you to know everything. Acknowledge that you don't know, then offer to get back to them with a response promptly, perhaps by email. Admitting you don't know something and then coming up with an answer later can be a great credibility builder.

➤ Dealing with Objections

There are two steps to dealing with objections: Validation + Response. The first relates to the fact that once an objection or hard pushback is aired, the tenor of the meeting may shift, inching away from a polite back-and-forth toward conflict.

To avoid that, your immediate task is to ensure that your client feels understood. This is "validation." A good validation avoids an argument. It doesn't mean letting yourself get steamrolled by giving a limp response. Your objective is to return to a normal discussion, and a good validation sets that up. One thing worth noting: You are not agreeing with the substance of the objection. You are validating that the objection is understood.

Here's an example:

Client: Your fees are outside our normal price range.

You: Of course. I completely understand that you've got a budget to manage. (Or: Absolutely! You need to demonstrate the value received for every dollar spent.)

Most people don't even try to validate, or do it poorly, with worn-out, meaningless phrases, like "That's a good question." But misusing or overusing that phrase can diminish your credibility, (or worse, sound ass-kissy.) To avoid that, try to make the validation as specific to the objection as possible. If you have thought through the tough questions beforehand, you should be able to validate without much trouble.

There's no need to drag the validation out. Your aim is to immediately pivot to your response, which will typically involve one of these strategies:

- Ask them to elaborate. This is my personal favorite, because it gets the client talking again and provides the chance to offer a better answer. For the best results, be your natural, curious self and perhaps ask for an example, or have them detail exactly why this is of concern to them. "You referred to a 'normal' fee range. Can you explain how you measure value received in programs such as ours?" Best to ask an open question so you get a more robust and informative answer. Let the client talk!

- Isolate their objection. "If we can fix this, are there any other concerns?" if they say no, then you know what you must solve for. This also has the effect of putting their (sole) objection in perspective against the upsides of what you are proposing. If I can isolate, I often follow up by asking them to elaborate.

- Go for a pre-empt. If you've anticipated the question during your preparation, good for you! Assuming you've prepared a solid answer, you have a decision to make. You can choose to address a potential issue before they have a chance to object (pre-empt), or decide to wait until they raise it to give your answer. Sometimes it's good to let them air their concern; other times pre-emption works best. There is no iron-clad rule here. Go with your gut.

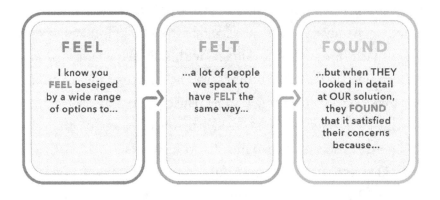

Another of my favorite techniques, which combines both the validation and response, is known as Feel-Felt-Found (above). This is effective because you are using the voice of other clients to respond. First, we validate to the client that we know how they Feel; the second part (Felt) assures your client that they are not alone, that other bright people have had similar concerns (this is called social proof, covered in detail in the next chapter). Finally, we tell the client what other clients have discovered, or Found (i.e., our response). A caveat: This is admittedly a well-worn technique. So while it's effective, don't use FFF more than once in a meeting, lest you sound like someone who just took a sales training class.

Above all, keep in mind that objections are not personal, though having one hurled at you can sometimes feel like a personal attack. That's a shitty feeling, to be sure, but remember, feelings aren't facts. The client is not rejecting you; they simply may not like what you're pitching. It's business. Perhaps you can make an adjustment and get them to reconsider. Perhaps you can't.

➤ Tips on Answering Questions Well

On several occasions, I've referenced the importance of pausing to emphasize key points, and to give people a chance to interject. Another effective use of silence is right after a thoughtful question is asked. There are several advantages to this. Even if you've answered a given question dozens of times, it's the first time the questioner has asked it of you. Taking a short pause before answering shows the questioner that you are considering the question. It's flattering and it gives you a chance to marshal your words.

I also use this 'thinking pause' to remind myself to answer directly (BLUF—bottom line up front) and, since I have a tendency to answer questions with stories that go on for too long, to make sure my answer is short. At Templar Advisors[35], we referred to the two approaches to answering questions as Cartesian vs. Anti-Cartesian, labels derived from the name of the French philosopher and mathematician René Descartes.

Descartes' academic background informed his (Cartesian) approach to presenting information. It's an information-rich framework in which all of the predicate details are presented as building toward, and in support of, the conclusion (or answer) at the end. Think of it as a math proof, where you "show your work," bringing the audience along with you until you reach the conclusion together. People with technical or academic backgrounds are more amenable to this approach. You will find this is also true with people who are skeptical of your conclusion or the thinking behind it. The problem with this approach is that it takes longer than the normal attention span in the business world.

In business (and, for me, in all areas), the Anti-Cartesian approach is favored: giving a direct answer first, followed by a limited number of supporting details that buttress your main point. Again, it's not necessary to show all you know. Leaving out some detail (without weakening or giving an incomplete answer) may elicit another question.

Here's an example I've used for years:

On a cold, snowy night, Jack and I pulled into the driveway after a day-long soccer tournament. Immediately, I noticed your mom's car was not there. When we went inside, I asked, "What happened to your car?"

---

[35] Templar helps businesses and individuals enhance every aspect of their communications with remarkable success. During my time there, I helped Fortune 500 companies across the globe improve client relationships, executive presence, financial presentations, and pitches by offering advice, training, and one-to-one coaching. It was not uncommon for clients to double their close rate in final presentations. Visit templaradvisors.com.

Cartesian answer: It was so beautiful when I got up this morning that I decided to go visit Sarah up in Argyle. But first I stopped and got Wolfie, and we went to the Blue Ribbon Diner for breakfast. When we left, it started to snow. You know that winding road that leads up the hill, right by Sarah's house?...

Anti-Cartesian answer: Ugh. I got in a little accident on my way to Sarah's today. Nobody was hurt. The police came, but I didn't get a ticket. Got the car to the shop and I pick up the rental tomorrow. Long day. Wanna get takeout?

Answers should also be short, preferably 30 seconds, but no more than one minute. Answer the question directly, provide any necessary supporting information, and then be quiet, or, if in mid-presentation, bridge back to what you had been saying.

CHAPTER 17

Cultivate Presence

"Presence is not so much getting people to like you as getting people to like themselves when you're around."
—*Robert Breault*

Having presence is mostly about you being you. Contrary to popular belief, gravitas is not a function of age or experience. The reason we tend to associate presence with older people is that the dominant factor of presence happens to be self-confidence. For most of us, especially early in our careers, we'd settle for not looking like we are scared shitless, never mind having presence. Happily, it's possible to develop presence and the key to doing it is in this book. Besides reading, all that's left for you to do is to practice.

Presence is all about the way you carry yourself and treat those around you. Broadly, it's about how others perceive you. To get a more concrete idea of what it means, let's look at some of the lessons I've laid out in these pages through the lens of presence.

Be present in conversations. When having a conversation, whether one-on-one or in a group, make an effort to actively engage yourself in the situation. You should refrain from focusing on what you want to say and instead show people around you that you are listening.

When you're the one speaking in a group, make an effort to look at each individual as you talk. If you're talking to one person, the goal should be to make them feel as if they're the only person in the room.

Don't be negative. A good way to be more likable is to stay away from negativity. No one wants to be around the guy who complains about everything. If you have a complaint or are pissed off about something, pick one person to vent to rather than venting to anyone who will listen. Don't be fake, but rather, learn to share the enthusiasm that others have in what they value and are passionate about, and ask questions that lead to a conversation with more depth and that brings the interaction between you and others into a more exclusive state.

Recognize positive contributions. Not everyone likes to be recognized in the same way, but the desire to be noticed and appreciated for good work and accomplishments is nearly universal. It's your job to figure out how to recognize each individual in a way that is meaningful to them.[36]

---

[36] When you guys were about 5 and 7 years old, the Cancer Society assigned me to work in Rochester for six months to help hire new leadership. The office was co-located with a Hope Lodge in what the Catholics who ran it half a century ago euphemistically called a "home for wayward girls." During the week, I would often work late into the evening because I still had my general counsel job to do, and because I wanted to leave early enough on Fridays to have a proper weekend with you guys. After hours, there was a janitor/night watchman named Mark who would stop by my office when I worked late. He was a super nice guy and, as I later discovered, an interesting dude. But by about his third stop and chat I began to dread the visits—they were all at least 45 minutes long, and I had work to do! What kind of weird-ass behavior is that? But one night, instead of trying to hide from Mark, I smelled the delicious aroma of baked goods and went to investigate.

Smile authentically. This means having a smile that shows warmth. Be authentic, of course, but practice! When you smile, people should be able to see it in your eyes and not just in your mouth (advice, incidentally, that makes sense in these mask-wearing times). You can spot a fake smile and so can everyone else. Make it a habit to greet everyone you meet with warmth.

Be well groomed. Invest in quality. Wear the best shoes you can afford, and keep them shined. Buy at least one suit (or outfit) at a high-end store so you can experience how much better quality workmanship feels and looks, and, most important, how it makes *you* feel. There is a self-confidence that comes with being well dressed. Superficial or not, appearance matters. What you wear becomes part of your image and influences how others perceive you.

Listen more than you talk. Presence is never just about being a good speaker. Listen intently, and see if you can put what you learn to use to enrich, help, and encourage others.

Don't gossip. No one ever made themselves great by gossiping about how small someone else is. Plus, it's a huge character tell. If you gossip about others, people will wonder what you say behind *their* back. I had a boss who once insisted that I "never say anything, to anyone, about anything!" He was clearly having an emotional

---

That's when I saw Mark organizing a pie-tasting party with half of the cancer patients/guests of Hope Lodge. I found out that he did this every week and paid for the ingredients for four to eight pies out of his own pocket. Mark, it turns out, was a humble old-school guy, and, as is often the case with humble people, his contributions were often overlooked. So, I wrote a letter to the CEO extolling his virtues, which I copied and placed in his personnel file, a move that went out of style ages ago. Shortly after that, Mark and I said our goodbyes and I left the Rochester posting. About a month later, two of my best mates called to tell me that Mark had memorialized my time there, and that next time I was in town, I should stop by my old Hope Lodge room. Months later, I did and saw Mark's handiwork: He had made a plaque that read "Patrick McKenna Slept Here" and mounted it on the door of my room at the Hope Lodge.

moment, but his advice stuck with me and helped me as a lawyer and judge, when keeping confidences was crucial to professional integrity. Be a vault. Set an example.

Show humility. The people I know with the greatest presence are also the humblest. They own up to their mistakes, generously share credit, and, most important, learn from their missteps.

Be a lifelong learner. Having presence is about learning new things and keeping yourself in tune with what's happening in the world. You can't really be an excellent conversationalist if you don't know what's going on. Strive to learn something new every day. Consider yourself a student, whatever your age.

CHAPTER 18

Be the Right Kind of Leader

I never became a great leader, but I had my moments. At the beginning of my career, I was so self-conscious that it made me a poor listener; I was too busy thinking of what I'd say next. Unfortunately, I habitually wore a mask of confidence that hid any humility I might have been feeling. I know I've advocated the "fake it 'til you make it" approach for habits and behaviors that don't come naturally, but there is a caveat: Faking while you are actively working toward developing a new habit is fine. Anything else, and you're just trying to fool others. This will make your imposter syndrome worse, because you are, in fact, being an imposter.[37]

The question is, can great leadership be taught?

---

[37] My parents met in graduate school at the University of Kansas in the relatively small Romance Languages department. My mom saw my dad walk through the classroom door "with a slight swagger" on the first day of class. She recalled thinking he was the most confident person she had ever seen. My dad remembers that moment differently. Your grandpa said he was never more frightened in his life. But John J. McKenna never let anyone see him sweat.

I believe it can, but it requires discipline and work in inverse proportion to your humility and your ability to listen deeply. Ironically, people with outsized egos and poor listening skills are often put in positions of authority, but they rarely succeed or are seen as great leaders in the long-term. One thing to keep in mind is the distinction between leader and boss. You can be in an entry-level job with no one reporting to you and still be a great leader. My core advice is this: Watch and learn from the natural leaders around you. If you can, and as early in your career as you can, work for and with people who embody *servant leadership*—a management philosophy that places people at the core of leadership, holds service to others as the ultimate act of fulfillment, and focuses on helping everyone to grow as people. If you emulate and practice the principles I outline here, you'll be on your way to a fulfilling career, even if you never nab the corner office.

Here's how I became aware of servant leadership (SL). When I worked at the law firm in the 1990s, I didn't have much opportunity to think or work strategically, except with a few forward-thinking clients. I was growing weary of solving the same problem over and over, without any sense of belonging or clear mission. As time went on, I heard other lawyers at the firm advise clients using the words, *"What you need to do is..."* while I would say, *"What we need to do is ..."* I yearned to be part of a team, to have goals in common, and my language gave me away. But I was just a hired gun, albeit a successful one, and it was getting old.

Then, in 1998, I was retained by the American Cancer Society to represent them in the Tobacco Settlement. During that time, I met many of the ACS leaders who were engaged in battling Big Tobacco. Together, we strategized ways to maximize political support for our position. I wasn't just litigating; I was fighting cancer! I was craving a sense of being part of a team; I wanted to be of service to a greater good, so I stayed in touch with my new friends, curious as to what my next step might be.

There were two especially sweet moments in that engagement. The first is that my little sis, the late great Carol Elizabeth McKenna, got my name in front of the ACS's CEO for consideration on the settlement work.[38] Later, Carol would remind me, usually when I was kicking her ass in backgammon, that she was still awaiting her cut.

The second wonderful thing was that I reconnected with Kathy Caggiano, a friend from high school. Kathleen headed up human resources for ACS in New York State. I did a little pro bono work with her, and she introduced me to the concept of servant leadership. She described SL as flipping over the traditional corporate org chart triangle, where leadership resided at the top.

It sounded radical. I knew Kathy Caggiano had a strong moral compass back in high school and was heartened that the grown-up Kathleen Caggiano-Siino not only kept that compass but paired it with a management philosophy perfectly suited to her values. I felt both envious and inspired to explore servant leadership myself.

I learned that in an organization that practices servant leadership, the "higher" up the chain you go, the greater your responsibility to support those who would have been "beneath" you in the old triangle. I also discovered the work of Robert Greenleaf, an AT&T research executive who published the seminal essay "The Servant as Leader." Reading Greenleaf's work and having further conversations with Kathleen led to my pilgrimage to Indianapolis

---

[38] A few years prior, Carol had been a single mom of two beautiful little girls, trying to get back into the workforce. She took a receptionist job at the Cancer Society. Her boss, Patricia Covell, recognized Carol's talents and began promoting her until she eventually became head of advocacy for New York State. They supported Carol's hard work, and she changed her life. That really caught my eye. I've been forever grateful to Pat Covell, Don Distasio, Dave Momrow, Jeanne Walsh, Lisa Currin and others for having my little sis's back.

in 2000 for a Servant Leadership conference. It was fabulous, but one afternoon I found myself in a plenary session with a pianist/ motivational speaker. I am way too curmudgeonly to put stock in such an admixture.[39]

Sensing a horrific train wreck, I hightailed it out of the conference room and headed to Starbucks. On my way back, I ended up walking past the room with the pianist. Briefly, I heard piano music. Then it stopped. I don't know why I lingered; all I remember is that 20 minutes later, I was in the back of the conference room writing and choking back tears. "If you don't play your music, who will?" asked the excellent Michael Jones as he led the group through an exercise to uncover our true passion.[40] What resulted was less

[39] I also inherited a sardonic sense of humor from my dad. Here's a quote he would have enjoyed: "I have a most peaceable disposition. My desires are for a modest hut, a thatched roof, but a good bed, good food, very fresh milk and butter, flowers in front of my window, and a few pretty trees by my door. And should the good Lord wish to make me really happy, he will allow me the pleasure of seeing about six or seven of my enemies hanged upon those trees." —Heinrich Heine

[40] On the flight home, I drafted a letter to Don Distasio, who had just become CEO of a major division of the ACS, following a series of internal mergers. In it, I urged Don to hire me as general counsel. It took months of meetings, but about a month after you were born, Jack, I got the call. I remember it well. It was Tuesday of Thanksgiving week, and the managing partner of the law firm had just taken me to lunch. During that lunch, I found myself hoping that he wouldn't pop the question about my becoming partner. I had joined the firm six and a half years earlier and had worked my ass off for that goal. Yet there I was, hoping he wouldn't make me an offer because I hadn't heard back from the ACS. It turned out that he hit the perfect note for the moment. He affirmed that the partnership was, indeed, open to me and that the partners wanted me to lead a certain practice area. He told me to give it some thought.

When I returned from lunch, my heart leapt at seeing the red light flashing on my phone. I returned Don's call and remembered falling to my knees in gratitude when he made the offer. And the salary was what I had asked for. It would enable your mom to stay home, which we both wanted. That Thanksgiving was the only time we ever went out. About 20 of us around the table. I remember your head nestled into my neck as I walked you into a nap, feeling like the luckiest man on the face of the earth.

a discovery than a reawakening of my aspirations from a decade earlier, when I had built my résumé around the objective of finding creative solutions to the problems faced by disadvantaged people. I had joined the law firm in 1994, right after law school and a year in the public defender's office, because I realized that the time for law firm work was now or never. I chose a firm where I knew and liked many of the lawyers. They were a wonderful group, but as it turns out, the traditional route was not for me.

Instead, I carved out a deal with ACS chief executive Don Distasio to serve as general counsel. To avoid falling back into the traditional lawyer role, we agreed that in addition to managing the legal function, I would also lead strategic initiatives that would directly advance the mission. I was about to get some on-the-job training in leadership, fighting cancer, and public health.

One early strategic project was to support Kathleen and her team in educating senior management about servant leadership and to help create a culture based on SL principles, which I've outlined below.

➤ Servant-Leadership Principles

I've advised you to gravitate toward and learn from servant leaders, and to fashion your leadership skills so that you discover how fulfilling service to others and fostering other people's growth can be.

The following principles, developed by Robert Greenleaf, are easy to understand intellectually, and to pay lip service to. But carrying out this way of leading isn't as easy as you might think. The qualities below take awareness and practice.

Empathy: Deep, empathic listening is at the root of all good communication and decision-making and a trait of all good servant leaders. It is not enough to rely on reason and the information in your head; we also need to rely on the wisdom in our heart. Good listeners get more information from listening deeply—and here's the important part—to what is said and what is unsaid. Servant leaders accept and recognize people for who they are, even when their behavior or performance needs to change, so there is no need for judgment to interfere with deep listening.

Healing: We all have a feeling of being less than whole. It can take innumerable forms: that we don't measure up intellectually, that we aren't worthy of unconditional love, that our physical bodies are imperfect, or insert any one of the infinite insecurities in the universe here. But whatever form these "less-than" feelings take, they cause a tremendous amount of pain.

Yet most people forget that we all have this in common. Servant leaders don't. They treat each person with respect for their humanity, blemishes and all. When we treat others like that, they feel less vulnerable and are more likely to treat others the same way. It's another virtuous upward spiral and is a powerful tool in bringing about cultural change.

As Greenleaf writes in "The Servant as Leader": "There is something subtle communicated to one who is being served and led if, implicit in the compact between servant-leader and led, is the understanding that the search for wholeness is something they share."

Self-Awareness: Self-awareness strengthens the servant leader and makes them sure-footed in ethical issues. It also strengthens them when questions about the use of power and adherence to values are in play. In times of trial and change, they don't need or seek reassurance because they are aware of and connected to their core values. Self-awareness is one trait that cries out for a daily discipline, as the servant leader will doubtless need time for reflection on whether and how their actions and plans are congruent with the shared values of the group.

Persuasion: To make decisions, give direction, and build consensus, servant leaders rely on persuasion rather than authority.

Strategic Thinking: As a leader, it's difficult to extricate yourself from tasks that consume so much time that it becomes impossible to pick up your head and look to the future. Yet to think strategically, you can't get bogged down in day-to-day activities and short-term gains. If all we do is act in response to urgency, regardless of whether the tasks are important or add value, we will never be proactive, progress will slow, and growth will stagnate.

To help you distinguish between urgent and nonurgent matters, I've borrowed the chart below from Stephen Covey, which illustrates why it's hard to move beyond day-to-day realities. Before showing clients this chart, I would have them make a list of every task they were responsible for. Then I would ask them to identify where each task belonged, quadrant-wise. Was it urgent or not? Was it important or not?

	Urgent	Not Urgent
Important	I **Fire Fighting** Crises Pressing problems Deadline-driven projects	II **Quality Time** Prevention, capability improvement Relationship building Recognizing new opportunities Planning, recreation
Not Important	III Distraction Interruptions, some callers Some mail, some reports Some meetings Proximate, pressing matters Popular activities	IV Time Wasting Trivia, busy work Some mail Some phone calls Time wasters Pleasant activities

What they often discovered is that they were giving shockingly little time to the non-urgent tasks of planning, improvement, and relationship building. Instead, they got stuck creating a last-minute report for their boss, who failed to provide sufficient direction at the outset. Or they'd end up canceling a stewardship lunch with a potential client because they had to put out a fire. Servant leaders shift the balance between day-to-day nonurgent tasks and longer-term strategic thinking by scheduling blocks of Quadrant II time and committing to use this time to update an outdated competitor analysis. It helps to make this kind of prioritizing a daily discipline. One hint: If you are not using the magic three hours I talked about earlier, these are ideally suited for Quadrant II activities.

Foresight: If you are lucky enough to be in a job that pays you to think, to succeed, and to fulfill your potential, you should strive to provide your best thinking. Does this remind you of the Desiderata maxim to stay interested in your career? Servant leaders use the lessons from the past, the realities of the present, and an informed view of the future to make sound decisions and clear, defensible future plans. Another benefit: When you routinize Quadrant II time and regularly do some informed thinking about the future, it's easier to stay interested in your career, however humble, because you don't get overwhelmed with boring busywork.

Individual and Community Growth: All leaders value individuals for their contributions. Servant leaders go a step further and demonstrate their commitment to the growth of each individual. This also becomes a virtuous upward cycle, creating empowered teams.[41]

---

[41] In *Good to Great,* Jim Collins defines the highest stage of leadership as a Level 5 Leader. His research revealed that leaders who achieve enduring success are distinguished by a paradoxical combination of personal humility and professional will. Respect toward people, thinking of others more than one's self, and a powerful commitment to achieving results are the traits that bring out the best in others.

Ultimately, being a servant leader begins with you. Don't wait for someone to come along and show you; servant leaders are too rare to risk that.

At the ACS, our CEO was a great man and a true visionary, and I've never met anyone who was better at assuming the best intentions of others. Unfortunately, the flip side of that positive trait is that it's harder to spot assholes.

So, while our CEO possessed an open mind, saw the value of SL, and was an authentic human being well along on the journey to becoming a servant leader, the ACS senior team did include one asshole who routinely made coworkers feel oppressed, humiliated, deflated, and belittled. On her recommendation, another bully, perhaps even nastier than she, was hired onto the senior team. In addition to being a kiss-up, kick-down phony, he did things like bring manicurists and tailors into his office to service him. And left his office door open so everyone could see. This at a fucking nonprofit, no less.

Hiring this guy was an unforced error, but it shows how much harm just one asshole in senior leadership can cause. The following story is a cautionary tale.

When Asshole #2 arrived at ACS, I was about a year into developing the Manhattan Hope Lodge, the single biggest and most expensive project in the company's history. This meant there were lots of contracts to be awarded. When Asshole #2 met me, he was all hail-fellow-well-met. My bullshit detector, which I inherited from both parents, went off immediately. Eventually, he casually mentioned that he could introduce me to architects and designers for the Hope Lodge as a way of, you know, "helping" me. My ass.

As soon as he realized that I wasn't handing out contracts to his friends when there were more suitable contractors, he did a 180-degree turn. From that day forward, I had a target on my back.

He continued to hector and undermine me every chance he got. It was not fun. He made dealing with Ken look like child's play. Still, I kept my head down and focused on the work. The daily discipline, which had lain dormant, was reactivated. *This too shall pass,* I reminded myself every day.

One Friday morning, I received a letter from an attorney representing a woman who worked in Asshole #2's organization. It contained the standard hostile work environment language and singled out Asshole #2. I didn't think much of it initially because although #2 was an asshole, he wasn't stupid, and there had been no red flags. Because I acted professionally and didn't jump to conclusions, I instantly became #2's best amigo. He mistook my calm demeanor for partiality in his favor. He told me he was flying to Puerto Rico that night to visit his sick grandmother (sniff) and that he would call me when he landed.

His effort to curry favor with me came out of the blue and spoke volumes more than any attorney letter. He WAS stupid, apparently, which made me suspicious. Late that night, the complainant's lawyer faxed me copies of boarding passes for adjacent seats on a flight to the Caribbean a month earlier for #2 and his accuser, a female underling. Over the weekend, it was decided that I would question #2 on Monday morning. I prepared two lines of questioning, one good cop, one bad cop, depending on how much of an asshole he was being.

Monday morning it rained so hard that umbrellas were useless, and everyone's socks were soaked after walking half a block. It created a dramatic tableau as the COO and I walked into the office at 19 West 56th Street to interview Asshole #2. It took about 15 minutes for this dumbass to paint himself into a corner. Yet he remained relaxed and smiling, acting for all the world like a wrongfully accused team player who would help us get to the bottom of this baseless claim. In response to the good cop questions, he declared that he had never traveled with the complainant in any way, shape, or form. I then handed him the boarding passes and watched the blood drain from his face and his eyes dart about, in a futile search for a way out. He had, indeed, engaged in an inappropriate relationship with someone who worked for him, failed to respect her desire to end it, and then lied to his boss about it.

Asshole #2 was fired on the spot. This story demonstrates how easy it is for an organization's culture to get hijacked by a small number of people. Changing a culture takes time, patience, and consensus on values. It doesn't happen overnight, with a meeting and a speech. True servant leaders have to be prepared to communicate with unstinting honesty about behaviors that violate shared values. This is one reason the work of the servant leader is so demanding.

Thinking about unstinting honesty brings to mind the story of Vice Admiral James Stockdale, a Vietnam veteran who spent nearly eight years as a prisoner of war in the infamously brutal Hanoi Hilton. Stanford business professor Jim Collins, fascinated by Stockdale's leadership during that time, interviewed the Vice Admiral for his 2001 book, *Good to Great*, sensing that Stockdale's experience might yield insight about what makes some leaders extraordinary.

When Collins asked how he was able to survive, Stockdale said, "You must never confuse faith that you will prevail in the end—which you can never afford to lose—with the discipline to confront the most brutal facts of your current reality, whatever they might be."

This became known as the Stockdale Paradox: Confront the brutal truth and yet never lose hope. Collins considered it to be a key characteristic of companies that were top performers in their sectors.

The brutal facts of my current reality are well known to me. Staying positive, putting on a brave face, and maintaining a sense of purpose are good things, but they don't forestall the inevitable. Marcus Aurelius bluntly said, "Death smiles at us all. All man can do is smile back." I see many people with ALS fight this disease—really do battle—to the bitter end, and I admire them. For some, success means living, or being cured. Sadly, many equate dying with failure.

Yet dying doesn't always mean failure.

When I was in law school, one of the veteran nurses from the Albany Medical Center Neonatal Intensive Care Unit (NICU) came to speak. When asked what the hardest part of her job was, I expected it to be the grief she experienced when babies died. Instead, she painted a different picture, one that gave us a clearer view of the world of a couple (or person) with a NICU baby. Every parent wants to go home with a healthy baby, the nurse said, pausing for emphasis and scanning the room full of people nodding their heads. So logically, she continued, "success" is reflexively equated with the child surviving. I mean the entire purpose of the NICU is to save babies' lives, right?

Sadly, she continued, some infants' lives are measured in hours and days, not years, and there is nothing medical to be done.

In other words, there are times when there is no advance warning, where the parent's expectations are so dashed that all they can focus on is the fact that their baby is going to die. The toughest and most important part of this nurse's job turned out to be working with those parents to redefine the meaning of success, amid soul-crushing sadness. I recall her giving an example by posing several questions: How can we make the time we have left meaningful? Is there music, or words the parents want their child to hear? Photographs? How do we express love or comfort the child?

Life is, indeed, a game of adjustments.

For me, this story underscored that great leaders are responsible for defining what success looks like for all the people they serve. Even in the direst circumstances, servant leaders begin with the desired outcome in mind, communicate clearly, execute calmly, and are present in a way that reassures those being served of a shared humanity.

CHAPTER 19

Listen Like Your Life Depends on It

Virtually everybody thinks they listen better than they actually do. Perhaps it's because the act of listening appears to be passive. I mean, who among us hasn't feigned paying attention in conversations, classes, or meetings? Just make eye contact, nod a bit, and half-smile at the speaker a few times, and you'll fool 'em every time.[42]

Try your best to not fake listen. Obviously.

Of course, good listening can be exhausting at times, since our brains process information far faster than people typically speak.

---

[42] Good listening is observable physically and verbally, but the physical signs and vocal cues tend to occur naturally when you're in the moment. The physical manifestations of listening include nodding, jotting notes, and maintaining eye contact and good posture. Another sign that we are truly listening is that we will repeat or paraphrase key points, summarize, and ask questions. To do this, to fully attend to the speaker, you need to suspend your own frame of reference, suspend judgment of the other person or their ideas, and avoid other internal mental activities. Your only job is to listen well.

That leaves us with extra bandwidth, within which we constantly battle little mental interruptions (*What time does the dry cleaners close? I can't forget to buy dog food tonight!* etc.). It's hard to stay 100% focused. But the rewards of mindful, consciously competent listening are incalculable and can be transformative.

Let's break this down.

Like all good things in life, good listening requires staying in the moment. It's not easy, so we have to be proactive about it. Our brains process so much faster than a speaker's rate of words that there is lots of unused bandwidth in any listener's mind, making them vulnerable to distraction.[43] You should not be surprised that the biggest distraction is rooted in the fact that we are all massively self-interested. That is:

> *"People don't listen to understand. They listen to reply."*
> —Stephen Covey

Sound familiar? There are lots of reasons we listen merely to reply: Nobody ever warned us not to; we want to appear prepared and smart; we're hoping to "win the point"; we've heard this question and think the answer we've given dozens of times will satisfy our counterpart, etc. But listening to reply is a bad habit, albeit a habit that is embedded in most of us. We can't listen deeply and process our reply at the same time, although it sure feels like we can.

A second common mistake listeners make is to answer too

---

[43] No, it is not possible to multitask. As of this writing, a summary of research examining multitasking on the American Psychological Association's website describes how so-called multitasking is neither effective nor efficient. These findings have demonstrated that when you shift focus from one task to another, that transition is neither fast nor smooth. Instead, there is a lag time during which your brain must yank itself from the initial task and then glom onto the new task. This shift, though it feels instantaneous, takes time. In fact, up to 40 percent more time than single-tasking—especially for complex activities.

quickly. Instead, when faced with a question or statement your counterparty believes warrants your consideration, you should allow for a space, a silence, a pause between question and answer, between stimulus and response.

Throughout this book I've talked about the importance of pausing. When you take that moment before answering, you signal to the listener that their question is worthy of thought, of contemplation. You are valuing the question while subtly assuring the other person that they will receive a thoughtful, cogent answer.[44]

Silence can feel pretty awkward, especially in meetings. But if you can become comfortable with it, you will often find that the other person will fill the void, often with valuable information. Silence also demonstrates gravitas and signals that you have the confidence to not be rushed into an answer. Having the courage to stop and think speaks volumes about you, especially when you're in a situation where you are among the youngest in a group. Other bad listening habits to avoid:

- As my dad would say, "Button your lip and learn something." You can't learn anything when you are talking, so as a general rule, strive for your total airtime to be one-third of the meeting.[45]
- Don't interrupt. It's rude.

---

[44] Obviously, you don't need a thinking pause before every answer. To show careful consideration of the question "Where were you born?" would be weird. I promise you'll be able to tell which questions or comments really matter to your counterparty.
[45] One of the best major-gift fundraisers I've known, and certainly the bravest, is Angie Garvich. Angie once had a garrulous CEO who was talking too much during meetings with potential donors. One day she brought a stopwatch to an hour-long meeting. After the meeting ended with no progress made, she asked the CEO how long he thought he'd spoken. He replied, "Ten minutes." She showed him the stopwatch: 47 minutes!

If a client tells you a story about themselves, don't jump in with one of your own. This was my Achilles heel for a long time. If a client told a story about Halloween with their kids, I felt almost bound to tell them mine. I thought I was building rapport! What I was actually doing was shifting the focus from them to me. And the worst part was that once the client stopped talking, I lost an opportunity to ask a question and maybe understand them better. Yes, it might make sense to share my story at some point, just not then.

- Don't have your phone visible or computer screen active. We know it's impolite to play with our phones when conversing, so we put them down and even turn them facedown to signal our virtue. That's not enough. In a study published in the *Journal of Social and Personal Relationships*, researchers found that the mere presence of a mobile phone on a table diminishes relationship quality compared to when the phone is absent. Participants in the presence of a phone also perceived less empathy from their partner and trusted them less. So turn the phone off and get it out of the client's sight.
- Remember to ask questions. Both reflective questions (which clarify what's been said) and probing questions (which deepen the conversation) are hallmarks of active listening.

The better the quality of the information you obtain from your client, the better you will understand not only what the other person is saying but also the motivation behind their words.

When you plan your meeting, be sure to jot down your questions, thinking about what you want to learn and the information you need to advance your ultimate objective. The point is to draft questions that will spark conversation, listen well to that conversation, and get closer to your goal.

There are three types of questions. Each has its place and purpose. The first is an *open question,* which is used to get your client to provide a broad answer, hopefully packed with useful information. An example: *What is important to you?* By definition, open questions should not be answerable with a yes or no.

The opposite is the *closed question,* which is used to extract specific information. Example: *What are you willing to pay?* Closed questions often yield short answers like *yes* or *no* and quickly put the ball back in your court. They also tend to be overused. Without a sense of where you are going, and logical follow-on questions, closed questions can weigh down a conversation and make it feel more like an interrogation.

The third type of question is the *reflective question,* which is a follow-on to check your understanding of what your client just said. An example of a decent, open reflective question: *I'm not sure I'm clear on that last point. Can you give me a specific?*

In my experience, reflective questions are underutilized because we're not listening well. But when used well, they help you ask for more, probe, clarify, uncover, and reflect key ideas.

If all this seems like a lot to swallow in order to simply listen well, don't fret. True listening gets easy quickly because the personal benefit for you is that once you start listening to understand, you'll set off a beautiful upward spiral beginning with more authentic encounters, greater trust, and, ultimately, more meaningful and productive relationships both personally and professionally.

The reason you want to ask probing questions and listen carefully to the responses is to get as much information as you can and to understand what exactly your counterparty is trying to solve for. It's important to distinguish between positions and the interests underlying those positions, as you can see in the chart below.

FIND THE INTERESTS BEHIND THE POSITIONS		
Context	Position Statement	Real Underlying Interest
Pricing	"I need a lower price"	I have budget issues until July
Peace Negotiations	"We must possess XYZ territory"	We are too vulnerable otherwise
Terms of Service	"We insist you provide a local service team"	Our last vendor sucked at remote diagnostics

This is particularly important in negotiations. Sometimes your counterparty will reveal the underlying interest; other times, they may not offer up their true motives. Take the middle example above, on peace negotiations. At the Camp David peace talks in 1978, President Carter mediated a number of Arab – Israeli issues. One sticking point was the Egyptian demand that Israel return the Sinai Peninsula which Israel had taken during the Six-Day War in 1967.

Israel's publicly stated position was that they would not relinquish the territory. But even though they had begun building settlements (at that point, roughly 4500 Israelis had moved to the Peninsula) and Israel's only oil rigs were on Sinai, continuing to occupy the territory wasn't really in Israel's best interests, save for eliminating the possibility that Egyptian tanks, in a repeat of 1967, would be able to blitzkrieg through the area, putting Israeli defenses on their back foot.

All of which is to say that Israel's public position to not relinquish was only one of several ways for them to achieve their interests, which was simply not to be put at a military disadvantage. Because peace with Israel was important to Egypt and other Arab states (though only Egypt and, to a lesser degree, Jordan, were willing to concede that publicly) there were lots of ways to achieve a win-win agreement. In the end, Egypt got the peninsula and oil fields back, and a combination of demilitarization and early warning technology satisfied Israel's real interest—to keep its citizens safe from attack.

My point here is to emphasize the importance of asking good questions so you can focus on the *real* issues (interests) at hand and avoid a binary choice.

CHAPTER 20

How to Negotiate Like a Pro

All of us negotiate constantly. Some negotiations are easy (where shall we go to eat?) and sometimes there is a helluva lot more on the line. And when the stakes are big and /or emotion starts creeping in, many people feel discomfort with the process, sometimes acutely.

I've taught thousands of people to get better results through negotiation. At the beginning of each class I would ask for a show of hands from people who considered themselves to be good negotiators. I could count on my fingers the number of hands I saw raised over the years.

In addition to feeling like they suck at negotiation, the adversarial aspects of negotiating seem to amplify people's discomfort and cause them to procrastinate. Indeed, clients reported that of all the work scenarios they could think of, preparing for negotiation is where procrastination hurt them the most—getting ready for a meeting in which negotiation was required would be pushed off and sometimes not done at all.

Such a pity, because the only thing that lies between a good and bad negotiation outcome is preparation.[46] And while the advice below is no substitute for a good class where you can practice techniques, simply understanding and taking these preparation steps will help you immeasurably.

Why prepare, other than upping your chances of success? When you do your homework, you will feel less anxious and more focused. You will listen better and appear more confident, giving you an edge right off the bat. As you prepare, keep these questions in mind, and be able to answer them:

- What results do we want in terms of the relationship or deal?
- What do they want to achieve?
- What are their interests, concerns, needs? Do we have any of these in common?
- How will we bridge the gap? Reasoned argument, bargaining power, creative ideas or a combination?
- How can we increase our power? (Power is largely a function of the alternatives each side has if the prospective deal falls through.)
- What's our fallback (i.e., the least we'll take)?
- What is our target? What should we open with?
- What are all the pieces that need to be negotiated? Are they linked?
- Which issues are important to us? To them?

---

[46] Jackie—remember when we went to Play It Again Sports to sell them some of your old baseball equipment? You were 14, and I recall telling you that I would take you on the condition that you say no to the first offer, make a counteroffer and then remain silent. You executed the plan perfectly. Just as you executed the suicide squeeze bunt in the All Star game a couple of years earlier! I told that story at every class. People loved it.

- What concessions might we get? Give?
- What info do we need?
- What can we tell/not tell them?
- What assumptions have we made?
- Should we do this by phone, by Zoom, in person or via email? If we do it in person, should the negotiation be on our territory or theirs?
- Should we go solo or with a team? If team, who will do what?

Once you've done your homework and feel as prepared as you can be, keep these key negotiating principles in mind once you're in the proverbial room:

- *Always go first*—and go for more than your target. Unless you have no idea what the value is for what you are seeking from your counterparty, make the first offer and force your opponent to respond. This is called *anchoring,* and there's ample science that shows that as long as your anchor is not unreasonably high (or low, if you're doing the buying) the outcome will skew in your favor.
- *Never say yes to the first offer.* Enough said.
- *Mind your language.* Unless you intend to signal that you have room to move, don't use floppy language. Note the difference between "I was looking for around $70" and "I want $70."
- *Get comfortable with silence.* If the other side persists in turning the negotiation into a game of whomever speaks first loses, summarize the current state of the negotiation and then suggest that everyone take a break and that you'll look forward to their response when you reconvene.
- *Take breaks as needed.* (See tip above.)

➤ CHAPTER 21

Off You Go!

I t's mid-June of 2020, and for the past two days, ALS just beat the crap out of me and, by extension, my wife, Libby. Clearly, this disease waits for no man to finish his book at his leisure.

Last night, a helpful inner voice of clarity reminded me, not for the first time, that I was giving advice that I wasn't using myself. In this case, I was ignoring the Stockdale Paradox about facing the brutal facts of my situation. My editor, whom I adore, actually suggested this adjustment weeks ago when my submissions to her had fallen off.

"Write the last chapter," she said. "That way, if the disease catches up to you, Libby and I can publish it." I didn't willfully ignore Paula's advice; I believed there was time to cover everything on my list. Right now, I hope to live long enough to finish this, give it to you, celebrate Libby's birthday and our anniversary, and see a blue wave wash over us in November, after Jack's and my birthdays. It's a modest goal, yet no one knows precisely when the bell will toll.

But yesterday, in the midst of the aforementioned rough patch, I realized that was only partially true. For me, writing this book is a proxy for having an endless conversation with you both. It was, and still is, my Hail Mary pass to win a battle with a foe that will beat my body, though I will not concede spiritual death. ALS robbed us of time when we needed it most. But each of you, and your amazing mom, stepped up, and together we did the best with the time we had left. There is a bit of divinity in all of us. And all that is divine, remains.

> *"Well, maybe a fella ain't got a soul of his own, but on'y a piece of a big one...I'll be all aroun' in the dark. I'll be ever'where— wherever you look. Wherever they's a fight so hungry people can eat, I'll be there. Wherever they's a cop beatin' up a guy, I'll be there. Why, I'll be in the way guys yell when they're mad an'—I'll be in the way kids laugh when they're hungry an' they know supper's ready. An' when our folks eat the stuff they raise an' live in the houses they build—why, I'll be there. See?"*
> —*Tom Joad in John Steinbeck's The Grapes of Wrath*

> ➤ APPENDIX A

A Little Help From My Friends

Shortly after it became too difficult for me to work, I realized how much combined experience and generosity I'd come across in the relationships I was privileged to form along the way. So I asked a few of my LinkedIn friends a simple question, a task that also helped prevent the rising, senseless sadness I felt after my diagnosis from overwhelming me.

The question: *What do you know now that you wished you knew when you began your professional life?* The number of thoughtful responses was gratifying and humbling. Here is a sampling:

> *It is okay to sit still for a few minutes and not busy yourself with work or noise. You can just be. Breathe in. Thank the universe for this moment. You aren't being lazy; you are giving yourself a rest from the world's demands. Self-love goes a long way.*
> *—Christine Ridley*

> *First, it's all about genuine relationships. Not manufactured ones, but authentic ones. The harder the relationship is, the harder you need to work at it.*
> *—Maria Guyette*

Listen to the language you use to describe
your situation; it reflects your belief.
—Benita Zahn

Don't hurt people. Never take a gypsy cab. And
girls, never start shaving your thighs.
—Caroline Sommers

Touch it once. Get it done now. Do it right or don't do it
at all. Nothing is beneath you; work is its own dignity.
Don't quit, but don't be scared to move on to better things;
some things are unchangeable. All jobs have boring
elements, so count your blessings—literally, count your
blessings and be grateful. Happiness is a decision.
—Hugo Williams

Hire people who are better than you.
—Wendy Bellus

Use every opportunity to learn and make yourself indispensable.
—Davis Hinsley Cheng

Own your mistakes swiftly and without looking
to share the blame. Everyone screws up; it's what
you do next that people will remember.
—Kristin Judd

Do not be afraid of telling truth to power. Just prepare thoughtfully.
—Paul Conti

Don't base your opinion of others, or of yourself, on
somebody else's input. Make your own judgments.
—Stephanie

Always think, What would Patrick do?
—Tracy Oakland

Look at criticism as feedback. Digest, examine,
evaluate, and then decide to change or ignore.
—Christine Sixta Rinehart

I wish I'd learned to live in the present
and not race to get to tomorrow.
—Geoffrey Doig-Marx

Dump the self-doubt.
—Ann MacAffer

Never pass up a good chance to help someone
or say something nice about someone.
—Dave Baker

➤ APPENDIX B

Finding Great Mentors

These pages contain a collection of the best advice I've seen on mentorship. Karen Burns, the author of *The Amazing Adventures of Working Girl: Real-Life Career Advice You Can Actually Use,* did a great job cogently laying out these pointers:

- As with any undertaking, begin with the end in mind. Your objective is not simply to get someone to say yes so you can check "Get a mentor" off your career-development checklist.
- Be clear on why you want a mentor. Are you looking for someone to offer specific advice? Do you want a conduit to your industry's movers and shakers? Or do you just need a sounding board?
- A mentor is a powerful role model. Look for someone who has the kind of life and work you'd like to have. Also, choose a mentor you truly respect. Don't just go for the biggest name you can find. Many mentors derive pleasure from "molding" someone in their own image—great for them and great for you if you want to be molded. But beware of mentors who are too bossy, controlling, or judgmental. This is your path, not theirs.

- Before asking someone to be your mentor, do a dry run. Simply ask for input on a single specific topic and see how that goes. Was their advice good? Was it delivered in a way that made sense to you and filled you with confidence and energy?

- When asking someone to be your mentor, explain why you're asking and what you'd expect out of the relationship. Start small, though. Perhaps a breakfast every other month or so; you don't want to overwhelm. Your mentors, unless retired, are likely busy. Name your reasons for approaching this particular person. Don't be afraid to be flattering (e.g., "I'm asking you because you are the most successful person I know.").

- Look for ways you can reciprocate the help your mentor offers. At the very least, you can occasionally spring for lunch or, say, send a fruit basket. You don't want to be all take-take-take. Show gratitude. Never let your mentor feel taken for granted! Also, supply feedback. If your mentor suggested something that really worked out for you, report back. People love hearing about their part in a success story.

- Consider getting two mentors. The main one is someone who doesn't work with you, someone with whom you can freely discuss workplace issues as well as your plans for future advancement. Think of this as a long-term relationship— and think beyond former bosses and professors. Look to older family members or friends, to your neighbours, spiritual leaders, community leaders, the networks of your friends and colleagues, or officials of professional or trade associations you belong to.

- You will doubtless need a sounding board at your job as well. Avoid asking your direct supervisor at work. Even in companies where there is an established mentor program, you should shop around to find a mentor you like, who is easy to talk with, and who will give you good, honest advice.

- Finally, if you ask someone to be your mentor and that person refuses, don't be hurt or offended. This is not personal! Potential good mentors are very busy people. Thank them for the consideration and ask for a referral.

➤ AFTERWORD

In late summer of 2017, I met Patrick via a mutual friend on Facebook. For the first month, he and I communicated only by text, and for the five months after that, only by text and telephone—not even video chat. Six months, thousands of pages of texts, and more than 900 hours of phone conversations later, we finally met in person. Across all those months and all those words, I not only learned that Patrick was a great communicator; I also learned more about Patrick than just about any other human being I've ever known. Just as important, Patrick helped me know myself better, too. On February 1, 2018, when he stepped off the plane in Denver for the first time, he was exactly what I expected.

The Patrick I got to know through all those conversations had three great loves: his children, Anne (19) and Jack (17); the St. Louis Cardinals; and his job. Patrick's work as an executive coach was both vocation and avocation; he had managed to find a job that drew on his skills not only as a lawyer and judge but also as an actor and, yes, a communicator. Patrick could stand in front of the country's most powerful and influential executives and teach them how to be better communicators themselves, as well as stronger negotiators, and more effective leaders. The enthusiasm he felt for his job, the energy he brought to it, were infectious. He lit up when he talked about his latest class or his most recent coaching client. He loved his colleagues, he loved what he was doing, and he was good at it. He told me that he had found the work that would keep him engaged and productive until retirement.

But during a visit to the gym in early November 2017, Patrick realized that the 20-pound dumbbell he had lifted only the week before was now too heavy for him to budge. He started noticing weakness in his left hand and crazy muscle twitches in his arm; he lost the fine-motor dexterity necessary to clip his fingernails, tie his shoes, and button his dress shirts. In December 2017, he was diagnosed with ALS, and everything changed.

ALS doesn't come with a handy guidebook, a timeline, a first this will happen, then that will happen. Our ALS Association case manager, Mary, told us that every person she meets with ALS is the first person with ALS she's ever met, because the progression of the disease is so unpredictable. ALS can begin as weakness in the arms or the legs, or as a problem with speaking or swallowing. It can progress rather rapidly—about half of the time, patients survive for less than three years—or not so rapidly: Twenty percent of patients survive for five to ten years. This not-knowing adds to the stress. Yet in some ways, Patrick was fortunate in that he at least got an immediate diagnosis. In our ALS support group, we heard the stories of people who were misdiagnosed for a year or more, undergoing unnecessary surgeries while doctors struggled to find the cause of their symptoms.

Given his love for his work, Patrick told his boss and colleagues that he would continue to work as long as he could. They were tremendously supportive, but over the next six months, he lost more and more strength in his left hand and arm, and his right hand also started to weaken. By June 2018 it was too exhausting for him to stand and talk for eight hours a day. He was having trouble operating the video recorder he used to tape and coach his students; even getting dressed for work was difficult. He was forced to retire much too early from the job he loved. It was heartbreaking.

Once Patrick stopped working, we had to decide where to live. New York, his home, was expensive, and my work, as a Project Manager for AT&T was in Denver. Colorado was more affordable than New York, and, as luck would have it, in 2016 the state had adopted a Medical Aid in Dying law, which allows terminally ill patients to request and self-administer life-ending medication. We had discussed what interventions, if any, Patrick would accept in order to prolong his life. A feeding tube? A non-invasive ventilator? A tracheotomy? At that point, he wanted none of it. He wanted to control his destiny and die as naturally as possible. The Medical Aid in Dying law would give him the flexibility to decide when he'd had enough.

By mid-2019, as chewing and swallowing became difficult and exhausting, Patrick began losing weight steadily, going from a healthy 5'10" 195 pounds to roughly 135 pounds over the course of the year. One morning, in mid-January 2020, I tried to feed him some yogurt, and he couldn't swallow it. I tried water. He couldn't swallow it. He could not get anything down his throat. I began to panic; not only could he not eat, but I had no way to give him any pain pills or other medications. That day, I begged him to accept a feeding tube. "I can't watch you starve to death," I pleaded. "It is horrible enough watching you die, but I can't watch that. Please." Finally, he agreed to let me call the doctor.

I wasn't sure it would still be possible for him to get a feeding tube: Once lung function reaches fifty percent or less (lungs are another victim of ALS), the surgery can be too dangerous; many doctors will no longer perform it. Had we waited too long and missed Patrick's window of opportunity? But on January 21, we checked into the outpatient surgery wing at Colorado University Hospital, and Patrick—by now down to perhaps 125 pounds—got his feeding tube. The access to nutrition allowed him to gain back a few pounds, increase his energy and eliminated the emotional and physical stress of eating and swallowing pills.

Why did Patrick change his mind about using artificial means to prolong his life? It wasn't only my desperate plea. The feeding tube also bought him time and energy to finish a project that, in the preceding months, had come to mean more and more to him: this book. He hadn't yet said everything he needed to say. He hadn't completed this legacy for his children.

A few months earlier, in November 2019, Anne and Jack had visited to celebrate Patrick's fifty-seventh birthday. Seeing their father inhabiting this unfamiliar body was jarring for both of them, I think; it's one thing to know that your father has a terminal illness but quite another to see his deterioration up close. For two days, they had a wonderful visit. Patrick could still talk, and what they couldn't understand, I could translate. When they left, I think Patrick finally felt at peace.

Still, as Patrick settled into life in Colorado, he started thinking about what he could leave his children. He knew that his diagnosis meant that he would almost certainly miss all the milestones of their young adult lives: college graduations, their entry into the work world, their first homes, their marriages and children. So, shortly after their visit, Patrick decided to write a slim booklet of advice to share the lessons he had learned in this life. He wanted to guide them as they entered the adult world, to keep himself alive as the voice they could turn to when they had those "I-really-wish -dad-were-here-so-I-could-ask-him. . . " moments. He wanted to leave behind a little piece of himself. At the end of November, his physical state waning, Patrick got to work. Writing *A Few Things Before I Go* became his last labor of love.

With awe, I watched his dedication and tenacity as he used eye gaze technology to write for hours at a time, typing out every word with his eyes until he could no longer focus. Every couple of hours I would adjust his wheelchair, move his arms, cross his legs—whatever it took to keep him comfortable. The work was physically exhausting, and emotionally draining, too, driving home the realization that what he was writing would have to substitute for the conversations he longed to have with his children as they navigated adulthood. But once he started to write, the words poured out of him. Somewhere along the way, the advice booklet morphed into a full-blown book. Writing gave Patrick a purpose. Soon he was up each morning, parked in front of the Tobii Dynavox, writing like a man on a mission. Time was critical. Given his weight loss and his weakness, we both expected that the inevitable was near. I didn't think he would see 2020. But he survived long enough to finish.

Reading this book reminds me why I fell in love with Patrick. I found his brilliant mind and his wicked sense of humor irresistible. We laughed constantly, we challenged each other to explore things that were new and different, and we understood each other. He used to joke that we shared the same brain. As Patrick's disease progressed, we could no longer talk endlessly, as we had early on. Sharing a brain helped; often, I could correctly guess what he needed as well as when he needed it. For me, losing that ongoing conversation is the hardest part of losing Patrick. Reading this book, I still feel like I have him whispering in my ear.

—*Elisabeth "Libby" McKenna August 6, 2020*

> ACKNOWLEDGMENTS

This book might not have been written if not for my former colleague and friend, Jennifer Schell-Podoll.[47] It was Jenn-Jenny who knew a gal, who knew a gal, who found the person who became my editor. I owe a lot to Jenn. She was the chief marketing and communication person on all the big projects at ACS, including my own. The thing is, I fancied myself a marketer at heart, and when we worked on the Manhattan Hope Lodge, a BFD, I envisioned a dynamic duo type of partnership ... two great marketing minds, etc. It wasn't until Jennifer executed a beautiful "difficult conversation" with me that I learned that my tendency to try to do her job was literally giving her nightmares. We both (well, not both, just me) made adjustments and from that day forward the best professional relationship I've ever had blossomed. We became fast friends, as well. She exemplifies the very best traits of a spiritual soul on a human journey. Everyone loves J-Po, but apart from her amazing husband Steve, I like to think I love her the best. I'll always remember when we held the Grand Opening for Hope Lodge, when the Broadway star I slated to sing cancelled two hours before the event. Jenn arranged for Steve,

---

[47] When I gave my farewell speech at the American Cancer Society, I had an entire page of notes about my respect and fondness for Jenn. But because that page got stuck to the page on top of it (and because I didn't number my pages), I ended up leaving her out. It wasn't until I sat back down, and Jennifer commandeered the microphone that I realized my tragic omission. Shiiiiit! She was gracious about it, but never stopped needling me about it. So she comes first this time.

a singer with an operatic voice, to fill in. He killed, and the Schell-Podolls saved my bacon. Thanks again, Steve.

Next up is my editor, Paula Derrow, who took this project on like it was her own. It must have been a challenge since we couldn't have a conversation except by text and email, but she was perfect. Because of this disease, there were days, weeks even, when I wasn't writing. Paula knew the realities of the situation and would patiently nudge and coax me back on track. And I know damn well that she undercharged me! Paula got my voice immediately and was a superb strategist as well as terrific editor. We became pals quickly. So much credit goes to her for this capstone project, I feel a bit sheepish being credited as sole author. It feels like our book as much as mine. Thank you, Paula, with all my heart. Also grateful you enlisted Marli Higa to copy edit. She did a great job and was likewise encouraging and nice to work with.

Isn't the cover beautiful? That's because I was blessed with the friendship of the immensely talented Rebecca Yaffe. I had no idea she was a graphic designer, among many other talents. It's funny the things that stick in your mind. I met Rebecca when I moved to Denver three years ago. I only knew her a little when my wife Libby and I were invited to speak at an ALS Association dinner. It was my first big social event in a wheelchair, and I was a little uncomfortable. I recall being in a corner, waiting for the event to start, and Rebecca came over to chat. She knelt down in her cocktail dress like it was the most natural thing in the world, so we could speak at eye level. It was breathtakingly thoughtful. And when she offered to take on the design for this book, I had zero trepidation. I wanted someone with her sensitivity to have her fingerprints all over this. Thank you for your steadfast support and immense talent, Rebecca. And above all, thank you for your friendship.

I don't think I would have crossed the finish line without the superb medical care I received in New York and Denver. While there isn't a goddamn thing docs can do to cure or extend life with ALS, both of my doctors, Mathew Harms at Columbia, and Mathew Wicklund at the University of Colorado, and their respective teams, were fabulous. When the time came, Bridges Hospice, especially our new, dear friend, Colette Graves, brought comfort and laughter to my final months. Thanks. Colette.

There are a slew of people who offered encouragement and support along the way. But, of course, my biggest cheerleader has been my wife, Elisabeth. People, this amazing woman married me AFTER I was diagnosed with Lou Gehrig's Disease! Who does that? More than anything or anyone, Libby makes me understand what Lou Gehrig meant in his farewell speech about having caught a tough break, but still feeling like the luckiest man in the world. Her support at every turn has kept me going. I love you, Libby.

I lost my ability to write or type months before I started writing. So, this book would have literally not been possible without the eyegaze technology introduced to me by the awesome Renée Karantunis and her team of speech and language pathologists. I didn't think writing a book of this size was possible, given that I couldn't type, but Renée and her crack staff set me up for success, and removed every technical obstacle. I don't know if I've ever seen an operation run more smoothly and with such a universally can-do attitude.

Now we move into territory where I begin to fear that I'm leaving someone out. There were a few people who made it their business to keep in touch and provide me with fun distractions, like movie clips and recommendations, funny memes, Gifs and general cheerleading. This group includes Laura Stedman, Mike Smalls, Brendan Cooney, Teri-Lynn Genovesi, Dave Stevens, Takani Aizeki, Rob Ventre, my brothers, Andrew and Brian, and my brothers-in-law, Ben and Adam Trissel. And in the position of honor, my patient and caring mother-in-law, Debby. Thank you. You guys kept me going.

In a special category are my friends from Templar Advisors, Charlie Garnett, Hugo Williams, Joe Bikart, James Patrick, Ian Fountain and Michelle Margolin. Templar was where all my strengths and passions converged. My work with this most generous group provided the basis for much of the contents of this book.

Last, I want to acknowledge Caroline Sommers and Sarah Cooper for taking the time to read, give feedback and write nice things for the back cover. They found this time amid a pandemic, a mitzvah that is not lost on me. Thank you, and much love to you both.

➤ THE BOOKSHELF: WORKS CONSULTED AND RECOMMENDED

Baron, Eric. *Innovative Team Selling: How to Leverage Your Resources and Make Team Selling Work.* Wiley, 2013.

Burns, Karen. *The Amazing Adventures of Working Girl: Real-Life Career Advice You Can Actually Use.* Running Press, 2009.

Cialdini, Robert B. *Influence: The Psychology of Persuasion.* HarperBusiness, 2006.

Collins, Jim. *Good to Great: Why Some Companies Make the Leap and Others Don't.* HarperBusiness, 2001.

Covey, Stephen R. *Primary Greatness: The 12 Levers of Success.* Simon & Schuster, 2016.

Covey, Stephen R. *The 7 Habits of Highly Effective People.* Simon & Schuster, 2013.

Goldstein, Noah J.; Martin, Steve J.; and Cialdini, Robert B. *Yes! 50 Scientifically Proven Ways to Be Persuasive.* Free Press, 2009.

Goodwin, Doris Kearns. *Team of Rivals: The Political Genius of Abraham Lincoln.* Simon & Schuster, 2006.

Kahneman, Daniel. *Thinking, Fast and Slow.* Farrar, Straus and Giroux, 2013.

McKenna, Andrew. *Sheer Madness: From Federal Prosecutor to Federal Prisoner: A Memoir.* CreateSpace, 2014.

Mitroff, Ian I. *Smart Thinking for Crazy Times: The Art of Solving the Right Problems*. Berrett-Koehler Publishers, 1998.

Patterson, Kerry; Grenny, Joseph; McMillan, Ron; and Switzler, Al. *Crucial Conversations: Tools for Talking When Stakes Are High*. McGraw-Hill Education, 2011.

Ryan, Richard M.; and Deci, Edward L. *Self-Determination Theory: Basic Psychological Needs in Motivation, Development, and Wellness*. The Guilford Press, 2017.

Brooks, Alison Wood. "Get Excited: Reappraising Pre-Performance Anxiety as Excitement." *Journal of Experimental Psychology*, Vol. 143, No. 3. 2014.

Deci, Edward L.; and Ryan, Richard M. (2012). "Motivation, Personality, and Development Within Embedded Social Contexts: An Overview of Self-Determination Theory." *The Oxford Handbook of Human Motivation*, Oxford University Press, February 2012.

Farnam Street. "The Most Respectful Interpretation." *Farnam Street*.

Friedman, Uri. "New Zealand's Prime Minister May Be the Most Effective Leader on the Planet." *The Atlantic*, April 19, 2020.

Langer, Ellen; Blank, Arthur; and Chanowitz, Benzion. "The Mindlessness of Ostensibly Thoughtful Action: The Role of 'Placebic' Information in Interpersonal Interaction." *Journal of Personality and Social Psychology*, Vol. 36, No. 6. 1978.

Lin, Helen Lee. "How Your Cell Phone Hurts Your Relationships." *Scientific American*, September 4, 2012.

Mayo Clinic. "Forgiveness: Letting Go of Grudges and Bitterness." MayoClinic.org, November 4, 2017.

Ryan, Richard M.; and Deci, Edward L. "Self-Determination Theory and the Facilitation of Intrinsic Motivation, Social Development, and Well-Being." *American Psychologist*, January 2000.

Silard, Anthony. "The Art of Pausing in Conversation: Your Weekly Wake-Up Call to Build Meaningful Relationships." *HuffPost*, May 2, 2014.

Weissmann, Elena. "How Phones Are Tearing Us Apart." *Psychology Today*, June 19, 2015.

White, Doug; and White, Polly. "3 Steps to a Well-Structured Presentation." *Entrepreneur*, October 18, 2016.

Wittreich, Warren J. "How to Buy/Sell Professional Services." *Harvard Business Review*, 1966.

➤ AUTHOR BIO

Photo by Joseph Schuyler

Patrick McKenna was born in Kansas, at the end of the Cuban missile crisis. He delivered newspapers, played baseball and enjoyed an idyllic childhood in Schenectady, New York. Along the way, he also became an actor, a lawyer, a judge, and finally a global communication consultant who taught Fortune 500 executives to negotiate and close colossal deals. He made lists in church basements and coached baseball.

The cost of living with Lou Gehrig's Disease trumps even the most resilient retirement plans. And so, like Ulysses Grant before him, Patrick spent the last few months of his life writing this book in an attempt to replenish the coffers and to express love and affection for his wife Elisabeth, son Jack, and daughter Anne.

Learn more at www.afewthingsbeforeIgo.com

CPSIA information can be obtained
at www.ICGtesting.com
Printed in the USA
LVHW080017121220
673921LV00007B/294

9 780578 779713